Communicating on Campus

Skills for Academic Speaking

Amy Hemmert
Ged O'Connell

Alta Book Center Publishers

Credits

Content Editor:	N. Ann Chenoweth
Production Editor:	Jamie A. Cross
Acquisition Editor:	Aarón Berman
Interior design:	Cleve Gallat
Cover Art:	Katherine Tillotson
Illustrations:	Jack McClean

Alta Book Center Publishers—San Francisco
14 Adrian Court
Burlingame, California 94010 USA
Phone: 800 ALTA/ESL • 650.692.1285
Fax: 800 ALTA/FAX • 650.692.4654
Email: info@altaesl.com • Website: www.altaesl.com

ISBN 978-1-882483-67-9

To Mike, Izumi, and the kids:
Megumi, Brian, Daniel, Dana, and David

CONTENTS

To the Student . . . . *ix*
Preface . . . . *x*
Acknowledgments . . . . *xii*
Components . . . . *xiii*

Unit 1: Meeting People on Campus 1

Chapter One: Getting to Know Others 3
Introduction 3
Practice 1: Introductions 4
Dialogue Analysis 6
Practice 2: Interrupting, Reporting Information 8
Practice 3: Conversation Starters 10
Practice 4: Taking One's Leave 11
Chapter Assignment: Getting to Know Others 12
Summary of Key Language 14

Unit 2: Getting Information on Campus 15

Chapter Two: Asking for Information 17
Introduction 17
Dialogue Analysis 18
Practice 1: Questions 19
Practice 2: Introducing a Topic, Thanking 21
Chapter Assignment: Asking for Information 28
Summary of Key Language 33

Chapter Three: Controlling a Conversation 35
Introduction 35
Dialogue Analysis 38
Practice 1: Checking Information 40
Practice 2: Seeking Clarification 44
Chapter Assignment: Controlling a Conversation 48
Summary of Key Language 54

Chapter Four: Active Listening Skills 55
   Introduction 55
   Dialogue Analysis 56
   Practice 1: Giving Verbal and Nonverbal Feedback 57
   Practice 2: Using Tag Responses 58
   Practice 3: Using Wh- Questions 59
   Chapter Assignment: Being an Active Listener 61
   Summary of Key Language 63

   UNIT ASSIGNMENT: Getting Information on Campus 64

Unit 3: The Teacher's Office 67

Chapter Five: Making an Appointment 69
   Introduction 69
   Dialogue Analysis 70
   Practice: Negotiating a Time 71
   Chapter Assignment: Making an Appointment 72
   Summary of Key Language 76

Chapter Six: Visiting a Teacher's Office 77
   Introduction 77
   Dialogue Analysis 78
   Practice 1: Opening a Conversation, Stating One's Business,
      and Closing a Conversation 79
   Practice 2: Providing Explanations 88
   Practice 3: Knowing When It's Time to Leave 91
   Chapter Assignment: Visiting a Teacher's Office 93
   Summary of Key Language 95

   UNIT ASSIGNMENT: Visiting a Teacher's Office 96

Unit 4: The Group Discussion 97

Chapter Seven: Participating in a Group Discussion................ 99
  Introduction... 99
  Dialogue Analysis 100
  Practice 1: Giving an Opinion, Agreeing 101
  Practice 2: Disagreeing Politely 102
  Chapter Assignment: Resolving Differences..................... 105
  Summary of Key Language 107

Chapter Eight: Leading a Group Discussion 109
  Introduction... 109
  Dialogue Analysis 110
  Practice 1: Introducing a Topic, Moving on to a New Topic 112
  Practice 2: Asking for an Opinion, Responding, Summarizing,
       Moving on to a New Topic 113
  Chapter Assignment: Mock Discussion 114
  Summary of Key Language 117

Chapter Nine: Reporting on a Group Discussion................. 119
  Introduction... 119
  Practice 1: Organizing a Summary........................... 120
  Practice 2: Preparing a Summary 122
  Chapter Assignment: Reporting on a Group Discussion 127
  Summary of Key Language 128

  UNIT ASSIGNMENT: The Group Discussion 129

Unit 5: The Peer Tutorial 131

Chapter Ten: Getting Advice 133
  Introduction... 133
  Dialogue Analysis 134
  Practice 1: Asking for Advice............................. 135
  Practice 2: Giving Advice................................. 136
  Chapter Assignment 1: Professional Advice 138
  Chapter Assignment 2: The Peer Tutorial 142
  Summary of Key Language 144

  UNIT ASSIGNMENT: The Peer Tutorial 145

Unit 6: Presentations 147

Chapter Eleven: Presenting Information to a Small Group 149
Introduction......149
Dialogue Analysis 150
Practice 1: Choosing a Topic 154
Practice 2: Preparing the Introduction 157
Practice 3: Preparing the Body......159
Practice 4: Preparing the Conclusion 160
Practice 5: Preparing Note Cards......162
Practice 6: Questioning a Speaker 164
Practice 7: Practicing Your Presentation......167
Chapter Assignment: Presenting Information to a Small Group......169
Summary of Key Language 171

Chapter Twelve: Demonstrating a Process to a Group 173
Introduction......173
Dialogue Analysis 174
Practice 1: Choosing a Topic 175
Practice 2: Using Visual Aids 178
Practice 3: Describing a Process......179
Practice 4: Reminding Someone to Do Something 180
Chapter Assignment: Demonstrating a Process to a Group 182
Summary of Key Language 185

Chapter Thirteen: Planning a Group Project 187
Introduction......187
Dialogue Analysis 188
Practice 1: Making Suggestions 190
Practice 2: Volunteering to Help 191
Practice 3: Asking for Volunteers......194
Chapter Assignment: Planning a Group Project......199
Summary of Key Language 202

UNIT ASSIGNMENT: The Group Project 203

Index of Key Language 205

TO THE STUDENT

Welcome to *Communicating on Campus!* In this course you will learn the skills necessary for successful communication at any university, college, school, or institute where English is spoken. You will learn about the social and cultural expectations of campus life, and you will learn specific expressions to help you communicate your ideas clearly and politely. Although this book provides opportunities for you to listen to spoken English, its main aim is to provide speaking practice. Thus the speaking activities are many and varied.

At the end of this course, you should be able to:
- express your ideas effectively
- speak fluently
- speak with grammatical accuracy
- speak politely
- find and correct your own mistakes

This textbook is made up of six units, divided into thirteen chapters. Each chapter is made up of four parts: an introduction, a dialogue analysis, practice activities, and a chapter assignment. Units 2–6 conclude with a unit assignment.

The introductions provide background information about the skills you will learn. They will help you understand what each chapter is about and will help you identify what you already know so that you can concentrate on learning new material. The dialogue analyses, which present the key language in context, should serve as models and provide listening practice. The practice activities are lively and interactive, and will give you practice in specific communication skills. The chapter and unit assignments provide opportunities for real-life practice.

Here are a few suggestions for getting the most out of this textbook:
- Make sure that you understand the focus of each activity, and that you practice what you are supposed to be practicing.
- If your classmates stray from the topic, remind them to focus on the task at hand.
- Make an effort to use the language that is new to you. Don't rely only on the language that you have known for a long time.
- Participate actively.
- Be creative.
- As much as possible, review and use the language outside of class.
- Use the academic language that you learn in class to communicate in nonacademic situations. If you don't know which situations are appropriate, ask your teacher.

Finally, relax, have fun, make new friends, and learn as much as you can!

PREFACE

Communicating on Campus is an intermediate- to advanced-level ESL textbook, designed to teach the academic speaking skills necessary for effective communication at universities, colleges, schools, or institutes where English is the medium of instruction. It is intended for use in communication skills classes in English-speaking countries and abroad.

This book is student-centered, task-based, and demands active participation from all students. The primary goal of the text is to provide opportunities for students to build fluency and accuracy in spoken English through innovative, lively activities. To accomplish this goal, larger tasks are broken down into more manageable tasks and practice activities, which are focused and fun. These practice activities are designed to instill confidence, increase motivation, and provide a sense of accomplishment for all students.

Communicating on Campus consists of six units, each focusing on a specific aspect of academic life. Units are further divided into fully integrated chapters, which center around a linguistic as well as a thematic focus. The book is organized as follows:

Unit 1: Meeting People on Campus
Chapter One: Getting to Know Others

Unit 2: Getting Information on Campus
Chapter Two: Asking for Information
Chapter Three: Controlling a Conversation
Chapter Four: Active Listening Skills

Unit 3: The Teacher's Office
Chapter Five: Making an Appointment
Chapter Six: Visiting a Teacher's Office

Unit 4: The Group Discussion
Chapter Seven: Participating in a Group Discussion
Chapter Eight: Leading a Group Discussion
Chapter Nine: Reporting on a Group Discussion

Unit 5: The Peer Tutorial
Chapter Ten: Getting Advice

Unit 6: Presentations
Chapter Eleven: Presenting Information to a Small Group
Chapter Twelve: Demonstrating a Process to a Group
Chapter Thirteen: Planning a Group Project

All chapters begin with an introduction and a dialogue analysis, followed by a series of controlled practice activities. These are designed to prepare students for the comprehensive chapter assignments at the end of each chapter. All units, except Unit 1, conclude with a unit assignment, which requires students to do in real life what they have practiced in the classroom.

Introduction

Each introduction begins with a cartoon that can be used as a starting point for a cross-cultural discussion of expectations on campus and in the classroom, followed by a short description of the chapter focus and an explanation of why students need to learn the skills presented in the chapter. This introduction provides a chapter context without requiring students to read a large body of material. It allows students to find out what they already know so that they can concentrate on learning the skills that are new to them.

Dialogue Analysis

The key language for each chapter is presented in a dialogue, both in written form and on audio cassette. Each dialogue is accompanied by a short listening activity, such as a highlighting or cloze exercise, which focuses the students' attention on the key language for that chapter. Though much of the key language relates to specific functions, such as giving an opinion, agreeing, and disagreeing, it is presented within a larger academic context, such as participating in a group discussion. This presentation of language in context not only serves as a model for what may be expected in campus life, but also promotes an awareness of socio-linguistic appropriateness and correct grammatical usage. While some of the dialogues are "academic," others are more light-hearted, allowing for further enjoyment and reduced classroom anxiety.

Practice Activities

Each chapter provides opportunity for practice through a wide variety of practice activities. The aim of these activities is to build both fluency and grammatical accuracy through repetition and practice. They demand a high degree of student involvement and physical movement. Tasks are student-centered, requiring participation in pairs, small groups, or as a whole class. They are designed to prepare students for the real-life activities presented at the end of each unit and ultimately for communication in an academic setting.

Chapter and Unit Assignments

The chapter and unit assignments vary to a great extent, ranging from role plays to real-life out-of-class speaking assignments. These activities serve as a final bridge between the practice activities and the students' actual on-campus experiences. The aim of the chapter and unit assignments is to build confidence and to demonstrate to students that they have mastered the key language.

ACKNOWLEDGMENTS

We are grateful to the following people for their help in producing this book:

Ann Chenoweth for her careful editing of the manuscript and for her valuable insights.

Jack McClean for his artistic creativity.

Ken Enochs, Patricia Galien, Nanci Graves, and Tony Mills for their help and advice in making the tape.

Aaron Berman and the rest of the staff at Alta Books for their expertise and encouragement in getting the book to press.

We are also grateful to all the teachers and students who helped us to pilot these materials.

COMPONENTS

Teacher's Guide

As *Communicating on Campus* is a student-centered course, the role of the teacher should be that of a facilitator, rather than a lecturer. In support of this role, the student's book is accompanied by a teacher's guide that is well-organized and easy to use. It contains reproducible cards and worksheets, which are necessary to do all of the activities in the student's book, as well as teaching suggestions, answer keys, and tapescripts, which allow for easy and thorough class preparation. The answers, presented in an easy-to-read form, enable teachers to review answers in class and to facilitate effective class discussions.

Audio Cassette

The audio cassette that accompanies *Communicating on Campus* contains recordings of all dialogues and other listening activities presented in the book. These provide students with listening input and exposure to a variety of English dialects.

Icon Key

 Fluency Circles

 Groupwork

 Highlighting

 Listening

 Mingle

 Pairwork

 Writing

UNIT 1
Meeting People on Campus

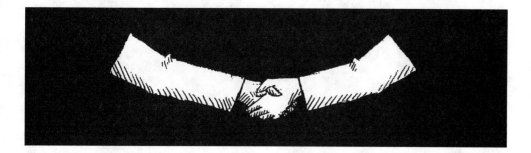

UNIT OUTLINE

Chapter One: **GETTING TO KNOW OTHERS**

Introduction
Practice 1: Introductions
Dialogue Analysis
Practice 2: Interrupting, Reporting Information
Practice 3: Conversation Starters
Practice 4: Taking One's Leave
Chapter Assignment: Getting to Know Others
Summary of Key Language

Chapter One

Getting to Know Others

INTRODUCTION

The types of experiences you have during your academic career will depend, in part, upon the relationships you form with other people on campus. The types of people you meet may be influenced by such decisions as the housing you choose, the activities you take part in, and the classes you select, as well as your attitudes toward meeting new people and your ability to do so.

Chapter One will teach you the skills you will need to meet new people and to feel more comfortable communicating with people you have just met. This chapter focuses specifically on introducing yourself to others, starting a conversation, interrupting politely, reporting information, and taking your leave.

Activity 1: Brainstorming

1. Make a list of the *places* on campus you are most likely to *meet new people*.
2. List three possible ways to *start a conversation* with someone you haven't met before.
3. What *expressions* can be used to *end a conversation?*
4. What differences and similarities, if any, have you noticed between the way Americans meet new people and the way people in your culture meet new people? In answering this question, you may want to consider the following:

   • How do people greet each other? (Do classmates greet one another outside of class?)
   • Is it considered appropriate to talk to strangers? Under what circumstances?
   • What do you do when you want to get to know someone better?
   • What is the relationship among students who are attending the same class?

PRACTICE 1: INTRODUCTIONS

The main purpose of Activity 2 is to get to know your classmates so that you will begin to feel comfortable working together. As you complete Activity 2, try to remember as many of your classmates' names as possible.

Activity 2: Class Mingle

First, think of *several* interesting things about yourself to tell your classmates. These could be interesting places you have been to, famous or interesting people you have met, or unusual things you have done.

Next, using the sample dialogue and expressions given below:

- introduce yourself to another student and find out where he or she is from
- tell that student the information about yourself
- listen to his or her information (and feel free to ask some follow-up questions)
- finish the conversation
- find another student and repeat the process
- take notes using the information sheet on the next page

Try to meet as many students as possible, and try to remember as many names and as much information as you can. If you want, you can give different information to different people to make the activity even more interesting.

Sample Dialogue

A: Hi, my name's _____. I'm Mexican.

B: Hi, I'm _____. I'm from China.

A: Nice to meet you.

B: Nice to meet you too.

A: So, can you tell me a little about yourself?

B: Sure, I've been to ten countries.

A: Wow, that's great! You must have had a wonderful time.

B: Yes, I did. Tell me something about you.

A: Okay, I survived a 6.1 earthquake!

B: Really? That must have been pretty scary!

A: Yes, it was.

B: Well, I really should mingle. Nice to have met you.

A: Yes, it was nice talking to you.

B: Bye.

A: Bye.

Key Language

Introducing Oneself

Hi. My name's ____ .

Hello. My name's ____ .

How do you do? My name's ____ .

I'm ____ .

Pleased to meet you.

Nice to meet you (too).

Name	City/Country	Interesting Information

 **DIALOGUE ANALYSIS**

Listen to the dialogue for a general understanding. Then complete Activity 3.

Situation: A young man enters a coffee shop and walks up to the counter where two waitresses are gossiping.

Waitress 1:	. . . and have you heard that Monica Smith who works in the kitchen has been married before?
Waitress 2:	Really?
Young Man:	Er, excuse me . . .
Waitress 1:	Not once, but twice!
Waitress 2:	No! Really?
Young Man:	Er, I'm sorry to interrupt, but . . .
Waitress 1:	And do you know she's been going to lunch with **another** man this week?
Waitress 2:	She hasn't, has she?
Young Man:	May I interrupt you for a few moments? Could you . . .?
Waitress 1:	Just a moment, dear . . . and not only that, but I heard she was old enough to be his mother!
Waitress 2:	Old enough to be his mother? That's scandalous!
Waitress 1:	And another thing, did you know . . .
Young Man:	Excuse me. I hope you don't mind me interrupting your extremely important conversation, but could you tell Monica Smith that I've come to take her to lunch?
Waitress 1:	Really? And who should I say you are?
Young Man:	Just tell her it's her son . . . from her first marriage!

5

10

15

20

 **Activity 3: Highlighting**

1. Using a highlighter, mark the expressions that the young man uses to *interrupt*.
2. Highlight the expressions that Waitress 1 uses to *report information*.

PRACTICE 2: INTERRUPTING, REPORTING INFORMATION

The purpose of Activity 4 is to practice interrupting politely and reporting information you have heard. These skills will help you to join in conversations more easily and to keep conversations moving.

 Activity 4: Class Mingle

In this activity you should gossip about your classmates, using the information you gathered in Activity 2. At times you will be a "gossiper" and at times you will be an "interrupter." Each time you change roles, put a ✓ on your scorecard in the appropriate column. For each role, follow the instructions below.

GOSSIPER

- Continue a conversation for as long as possible, using your notes from Activity 2.
- When another student interrupts, ignore that person and continue the conversation.
- When the interrupter has used at least three different expressions, allow him or her to interrupt your conversation.
- The last student to speak should leave the group to find another pair of students to politely interrupt.

> *Reporting Information*
> Have you heard (that) . . . ?
> Did you hear (that) . . . ?
> Do you know (that) . . . ?
> Did you know (that) . . . ?
> I heard (that) . . .

INTERRUPTER

- Find a pair of students who are having a conversation and interrupt them.
- They will try to ignore you; however, you should be persistent.
- Keep using different expressions until you finally succeed in interrupting them.

> *Interrupting*
> Excuse me . . .
> Excuse me for interrupting, but . . .
> I'm sorry to interrupt, but . . .
> May I interrupt you for a moment?
> Excuse me. I hope you don't mind me interrupting, but . . .

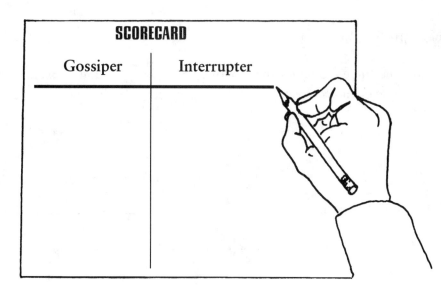

Sample Dialogue

Student 1:	Did you know that Jessica survived a 6.1 earthquake?
Student 2:	No, I didn't. That's amazing! She must have been awfully scared!
Student 1:	Yes, she said she was.
Student 3:	Excuse me for interrupting, but . . .
Student 2:	And did you hear that Philip has been to ten countries?
Student 3:	I'm sorry to interrupt, but . . .
Student 1:	Yes, and I heard that he's been to four continents!
Student 2:	That's amazing! I hope I can travel like that someday.
Student 3:	Excuse me. I hope you don't mind me interrupting, but may I join your conversation?
Student 2:	Okay, you two keep talking and I'll go mingle. Bye!

PRACTICE 3: CONVERSATION STARTERS

The purpose of Activities 5 and 6 is to learn how to start conversations. Activity 5 is a listening activity that asks you to identify types of conversation starters. In Activity 6 you will practice using conversation starters.

 Activity 5: Listening

In each of the three dialogues that follow, people are starting conversations. Write the topic of each conversation in the space provided below.

TOPIC

Dialogue One _____

Dialogue Two _____

Dialogue Three _____

 **Activity 6: Pairwork**

1. Look at the examples of conversation starters below.

Type of Conversation Starter	*Examples*	*Responses*
• **Talking about the weather**	Nice weather for January! It's an awful day, isn't it? It's a little cold today, don't you think?	Yes, isn't it beautiful? Yes, I hope the rain stops soon. Yes, but it's supposed to be even colder tomorrow!
• **Giving a compliment (+ a question)**	That's a nice sweater you're wearing. What a lovely dress! I like your earrings. Where did you get them?	Thanks, it was a birthday gift from my mother. You think so? I've had it forever! Oh thanks. I bought them in Hawaii on my last vacation.
• **Referring to a common situation**	Don't you find it noisy in the dorm? How are you enjoying the first week of school? This is such an interesting class, isn't it?	Yes, it's so bad I can hardly study in the evenings. It's fun, but I didn't expect so much homework! Yes, the instructor is really terrific.

2. In pairs practice starting a conversation by using expressions similar to the ones above.

Activity 7: Fluency Circles

To prepare for Activity 7, practice the following expressions with your partner. Remember to show disappointment about having to end the conversation so suddenly.

Key Language

> *Taking One's Leave*
> Look at your watch. Give a reason
> Mention the time. Give a reason   +
> Ask for the time. (Answer) Give a reason.
>
> { It's been nice talking with you.
>   It's been a pleasure talking with you.
>   I've really enjoyed talking with you.

- You will be given a piece of paper with a conversation starter, some information, and a conversation closer. Read it carefully and remember what it says.
- Your teacher will ask the class to form two circles, one inside the other, and will assign partners.
- When you are told to begin, the students on the outside circle should start a conversation with their partners on the inside circle, give their information, and when the teacher says "stop," take their leave by using an appropriate expression.
- When all students have finished, the students on the outside circle will move clockwise one space, and the activity will continue with new partners.
- The activity will then be repeated with the students on the inside circle giving the information on their papers.
- Remember to use the appropriate language for starting a conversation, reporting information, and leave-taking.

Sample Dialogue

> Student A: Hi, Clara. **What a beautiful sweater! Where did you get it?**
> Student B: Oh, thanks. I bought it downtown at the mall. It was on sale.
> Student A: I really love the color.
> Student B: Thanks!
> Student B: Hey listen, **did you hear that Pat's sister had a baby boy last night?**
> Student A: No I didn't. That's great news! What did they name him?
> Student B: Brian. Isn't that a great name?
> Student A: Yes. I can't wait to see a picture of him.
> Student B: Me neither. I bet he's adorable.
> Student A: Yes, I'm sure he is. **Oh, it's 2:25 already. I have class in five minutes. It's been great talking to you.**
> Student B: Yeah. Thanks for the news. I'll see you in class tomorrow. Bye.
> Student A: Bye.

PRACTICE 4: TAKING ONE'S LEAVE

The purpose of Activity 7 is to practice polite leave-taking.

CHAPTER ASSIGNMENT: GETTING TO KNOW OTHERS

 **Activity 8: Role Play**

In Activity 8, you will practice using all of the key language from Chapter One. On the following page is a grid that represents a 12-room student dorm. The dorm is occupied by you and the other people in your class. Your task is to talk to other students in your class and to find out the names and majors of the students who live in each room.

- Read your role card and ask your teacher about any words you don't understand.
- On the grid that follows, write your real name and the major given on your role card in the box with your room number.
- Talk to as many other students as possible.
- Tell them information about yourself and the other people who live around you.
- **You may not** tell anyone else your room number, though you may tell which floor you live on.
- Make notes about the information they give you.
- When you think you know which room a particular student lives in, write his or her name on the grid.

- **Remember to use the appropriate language for interrupting, and starting and ending a conversation.**

To make it easier for you, here's a list of the 12 majors:

Biology	Linguistics	Chemistry
Medicine	Communications	Music
Drama	Physical Education	Economics
Physics	English Literature	Sociology

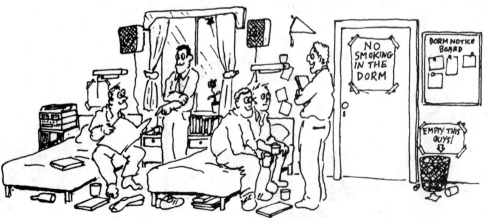

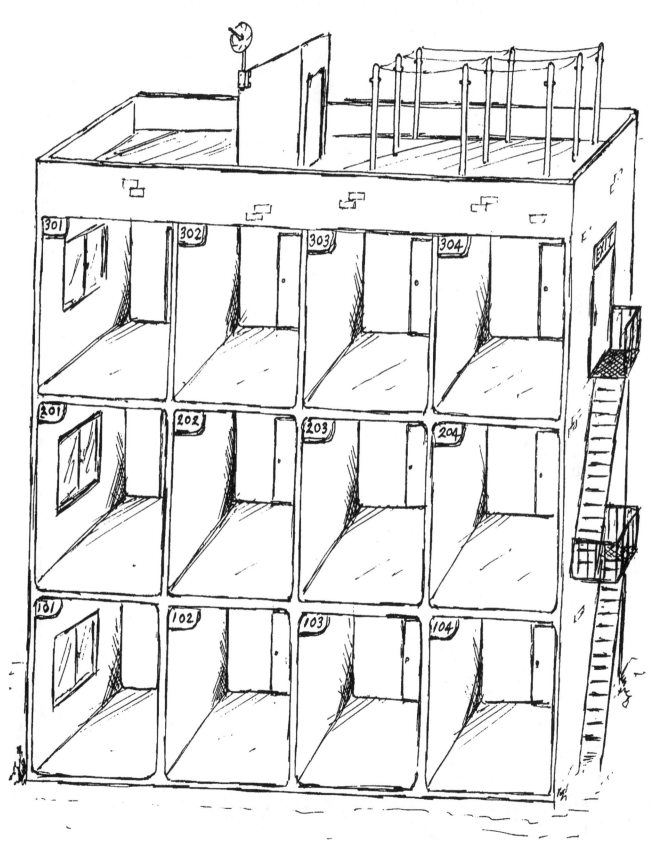

CHAPTER ONE: *Summary of Key Language*

INTRODUCING ONESELF

Hi. My name's _____ .

Hello. My name's _____.

How do you do? My name's _____ .

I'm _____ .

Pleased to meet you.

Nice to meet you (too).

INTERRUPTING

Excuse me . . .

Excuse me for interrupting, but . . .

I'm sorry to interrupt, but . . .

May I interrupt you for a moment?

Excuse me. I hope you don't mind me interrupting, but . . .

STARTING A CONVERSATION

Talking about the weather

Giving a compliment

Referring to a common situation

TAKING ONE'S LEAVE

Look at your watch. Give a reason.

Mention the time. Give a reason.

Ask for the time. (Answer) Give a reason.

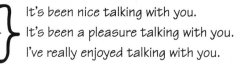

It's been nice talking with you.

+ It's been a pleasure talking with you.

I've really enjoyed talking with you.

OTHER

Add your own ideas for getting to know others here.

REPORTING INFORMATION

Have you heard (that) . . . ?

Did you hear (that) . . .?

Do you know (that) . . .?

Did you know (that) . . . ?

I heard (that) . . . .

UNIT 2
Getting Information on Campus

UNIT OUTLINE

Chapter Two: **Asking for Information**

Introduction
Dialogue Analysis
Practice 1: Questions
Practice 2: Introducing a Topic, Thanking
Chapter Assignment: Asking for Information
Summary of Key Language

Chapter Three: **Controlling a Conversation**

Introduction
Dialogue Analysis
Practice 1: Checking Information
Practice 2: Seeking Clarification
Chapter Assignment: Controlling a Conversation
Summary of Key Language

Chapter Four: **Active Listening Skills**

Introduction
Dialogue Analysis
Practice 1: Giving Verbal and Nonverbal Feedback
Practice 2: Using Tag Responses
Practice 3: Using Wh- Questions
Chapter Assignment: Being an Active Listener
Summary of Key Language

UNIT ASSIGNMENT: Getting Information on Campus

Chapter Two

Asking for Information

INTRODUCTION

Getting answers to the questions you have is an essential and often challenging part of academic life. Whether in class or in other places on campus, your ability to ask effective questions will influence the decisions you make and the types of experiences you have.

Asking for information usually consists of three parts: introducing the topic, asking questions, and saying "thank you." Introducing the topic allows the information giver to prepare for the conversation ahead or, if necessary, to refer the questioner to a person who can better answer questions on that particular topic. Asking appropriate well thought-out questions will help ensure that you get the exact information you need, and thanking the speaker makes the information giver feel appreciated. Chapter Two will teach you how to ask questions effectively in order to get the information you need.

Activity 1: Brainstorming

1. List the places on campus where you have gone to get information.
2. What kinds of information have you needed?
3. List some other places on campus where students frequently go to get information.
4. What difficulties, if any, have you experienced while trying to get information on campus?

DIALOGUE ANALYSIS

Listen to the dialogue once for a general understanding.
Then listen again and complete Activity 2.

*Situation: A new student goes to the library to get information about the library and its policies. She meets a man who she **thinks** is the librarian, but . . .*

Student: Hello. I'm a new student here at Camford University, and I'd like some information about the library. Do you mind if I ask you a few questions?

Man: No, of course not. I'm not very busy at the moment.

Student: Oh, thank you. First of all, what time does the library open and 5 close?

Man: Oh, the usual times.

Student: The **usual** times. Mmm, thank you very much . . . and er, . . . how many books can be taken out at the same time?

Man: As many as you like, I suppose. 10

Student: Oh, . . . I see . . . and . . . er . . . how long can I take them out for?

Man: Well, until the next person needs them, I guess.

Student: Really! Could you tell me what the fine is for overdue books?

Man: Well I expect it's quite a lot, but I'm sure they accept most major credit cards. 15

Student: Well, will the library get books and articles from other university libraries if requested?

Man: Mmm, I don't know.

Student: Well, could you tell me what the library policy is for lost books?

Man: Well, they'd probably ask me to find them. They ask me to do just 20 about everything else around here.

Student: I see. And, are you open on weekends?

Man: Yes, on Saturday but not on Sunday.

Student: Finally, can you tell me where the computers are?

Man: Yes, they're right over there. I've just finished cleaning them. 25

Student: You've just finished cleaning them? I thought you were the librarian.

Man: Oh, no dear, I'm the cleaner; the librarian's on his lunch break!

 **Activity 2: Highlighting and Categorizing**

1. Highlight all of the questions in the dialogue.
2. Divide the questions into two groups: wh- questions and yes–no questions.
3. Divide the yes–no questions into two grammatical groups.
4. What expression does the student use to introduce the topic?

Activity 3: Class Mingle

Preparation

- Sit in a circle and look at the next page.
- Write your own name in the large box at the top.
- Pass your book to the person on your left.
- In the book you receive from the person sitting on your right, fill in **one** of **the blank lines**. DO NOT write in any of the boxes.
- When you have finished, pass the book to the person on your left.
- Each time you receive a new book, fill in a different blank line.
- Continue doing this until your own book comes back to you.

Procedure

- Mingle with the other students in your group and try to find out which piece of information belongs to which person.
- When you find somebody who has written a particular piece of information, write his or her name in the box next to it.
- Remember to use only yes–no questions to get the answers for the top half of the page and wh- questions for the bottom half.
- Do not show your book to any other student.

PRACTICE 1: QUESTIONS

The purpose of Activity 3 is to practice forming yes–no and wh- questions.

YOUR NAME:

Yes–No Questions

Name of sister: _____

Birthday: _____

Parents' house number: _____

Favorite historical person: _____

City you would most like to visit: _____

Least liked food: _____

Wh- Questions:

Where you went for your last vacation: _____

Favorite film: _____

First foreign country visited: _____

Pet's name: _____

Most unusual form of transportation taken: _____

Favorite sport: _____

 **Activity 4: Class Mingle**

PRACTICE 2: INTRODUCING A TOPIC, THANKING

The purpose of Activity 4 is to practice using expressions for introducing a topic before asking questions, and thanking the speaker after you have finished asking questions.

- Your teacher will ask you to turn to a page in your textbook. Your page will have a grid with twelve topics, twelve questions, and six answers.
- Your goal is to find the six missing answers on your page. Some of the other students in the class will have your answers and some won't.
- Mix with the other students in your class until you meet another student. One of you should then introduce one of the topics, using one of the appropriate expressions listed below. If the other student has information on that topic, then the first student should ask a question in order to get one missing answer.
- When you have been given an answer, write it down quickly in the space provided, and thank the speaker, using one of the appropriate expressions. **Try to use as many different expressions as you can.**
- If the student does not have any information on that topic, you can say "Thanks anyway" or "Thank you anyway," and ask for information on a different topic.
- Repeat the activity with different partners until you have all the answers.

Sample Dialogue 1

Student A:	Hello. I was wondering if you had any information on the mountains of Antarctica.
Student B:	Sure. What would you like to know?
Student A:	Could you tell me what the highest mountain is?
Student B:	Yes. It's Vinson Massif. It's 16,864 feet high.
Student A:	Thank you very much. You've been very helpful.
Student B:	You're very welcome.

Sample Dialogue 2

Student A:	Hi. I'm Interested in European mountains. Do you have any information on that?
Student B:	Mmm. No, I'm sorry I don't.
Student A:	Okay, thanks anyway.
Student B:	No problem.

Key Language

Introducing a Topic	*Thanking*
I'd like some information on/about . . .	Thanks./Thank you.
Do you have any information on/about . . .	Thank you very much.
Could you tell me about . . .	Thank you very much for your time.
I'm interested in _____ . Do you have any information on that?	Thank you. You've been very helpful.
I was wondering if you had any information on/about . . .	Thank you for taking the time to talk with me. I really appreciate it.
I was wondering if you could tell me about . . .	Thanks anyway./Thank you anyway.

Activity 4: STUDENT A

TOPICS	QUESTIONS	ANSWERS
1. The Earth's Oceans	the largest ocean	Pacific Ocean 63,855,000 sq. mi.
2. The Earth's Islands	the largest island	Greenland 840,000 sq. mi.
3. South American Mountains	the highest mountain	
4. The Earth's Lakes	the largest lake	Caspian 152,084 sq. mi.
5. The Earth's Age	its approximate age	
6. North American Mountains	the highest mountain	
7. The Earth's Seas	the smallest of the great seas	
8. The Earth's Orbit	the speed at which it revolves around the sun	66,700 mph
9. The Earth's Rivers	the three longest rivers	the Nile, the Amazon, and the Mississippi
10. U.S. Cities	the largest city	
11. The Earth's Temperature	the highest recorded temperature	136.4°F
12. The Earth's Surface	the equatorial diameter	

Note:
sq. mi. = square miles
mph = miles per hour
°F = degrees Fahrenheit

Activity 4: STUDENT B

TOPICS	QUESTIONS	ANSWERS
1. The Earth's Oceans	the largest ocean	Pacific Ocean 63,855,000 sq. mi.
2. The Earth's Islands	the largest island	Greenland 840,000 sq. mi.
3. South American Mountains	the highest mountain	
4. The Earth's Lakes	the largest lake	
5. The Earth's Age	its approximate age	4.5 billion years
6. North American Mountains	the highest mountain	
7. The Earth's Seas	the smallest of the great seas	Baltic Sea 163,000 sq. mi.
8. The Earth's Orbit	the speed at which it revolves around the sun	
9. The Earth's Rivers	the three longest rivers	
10. U.S. Cities	the largest city	New York, New York
11. The Earth's Temperature	the highest recorded temperature	136.4°F
12. The Earth's Surface	the equatorial diameter	

Note:
sq. mi. = square miles
mph = miles per hour
°F = degrees Fahrenheit

Activity 4: STUDENT C

TOPICS	QUESTIONS	ANSWERS
1. The Earth's Oceans	the largest ocean	
2. The Earth's Islands	the largest island	Greenland 840,000 sq. mi.
3. South American Mountains	the highest mountain	Aconcagnua 22,831 feet
4. The Earth's Lakes	the largest lake	
5. The Earth's Age	its approximate age	
6. North American Mountains	the highest mountain	
7. The Earth's Seas	the smallest of the great seas	Baltic Sea 163,000 sq. mi.
8. The Earth's Orbit	the speed at which it revolves around the sun	66,700 mph
9. The Earth's Rivers	the three longest rivers	
10. U.S. Cities	the largest city	
11. The Earth's Temperature	the highest recorded temperature	136.4°F
12. The Earth's Surface	the equatorial diameter	7,926.68 miles

Note:
sq. mi. = square miles
mph = miles per hour
°F = degrees Fahrenheit

Activity 4: **STUDENT D**

TOPICS	QUESTIONS	ANSWERS
1. The Earth's Oceans	the largest ocean	
2. The Earth's Islands	the largest island	
3. South American Mountains	the highest mountain	Aconcagua 22,831 feet
4. The Earth's Lakes	the largest lake	Caspian 152,084 sq. mi.
5. The Earth's Age	its approximate age	
6. North American Mountains	the highest mountain	Mount McKinley 20,320 feet
7. The Earth's Seas	the smallest of the great seas	
8. The Earth's Orbit	the speed at which it revolves around the sun	
9. The Earth's Rivers	the three longest rivers	the Nile, the Amazon, and the Mississippi
10. U.S. Cities	the largest city	New York, New York
11. The Earth's Temperature	the highest recorded temperature	
12. The Earth's Surface	the equatorial diameter	7,926.68

Note:
sq. mi. = square miles
mph = miles per hour
°F = degrees Fahrenheit

Activity 4: STUDENT E

TOPICS	QUESTIONS	ANSWERS
1. The Earth's Oceans	the largest ocean	Pacific Ocean 63,855,000 sq. mi.
2. The Earth's Islands	the largest island	
3. South American Mountains	the highest mountain	
4. The Earth's Lakes	the largest lake	Caspian 152,084 sq. mi.
5. The Earth's Age	its approximate age	4.5 billion years
6. North American Mountains	the highest mountain	Mount McKinley 20,320 feet
7. The Earth's Seas	the smallest of the great seas	
8. The Earth's Orbit	the speed at which it revolves around the sun	66,700 mph
9. The Earth's Rivers	the three longest rivers	
10. U.S. Cities	the largest city	
11. The Earth's Temperature	the highest recorded temperature	
12. The Earth's Surface	the equatorial diameter	7,926.68

Note:
sq. mi. = square miles
mph = miles per hour
°F = degrees Fahrenheit

Activity 4: STUDENT F

TOPICS	QUESTIONS	ANSWERS
1. The Earth's Oceans	the largest ocean	
2. The Earth's Islands	the largest island	
3. South American Mountains	the highest mountain	Aconcagua 22,831 feet
4. The Earth's Lakes	the largest lake	
5. The Earth's Age	its approximate age	4.5 billion years
6. North American Mountains	the highest mountain	Mount McKinley 20,320 feet
7. The Earth's Seas	the smallest of the great seas	Baltic Sea 163,000 sq. mi.
8. The Earth's Orbit	the speed at which it revolves around the sun	
9. The Earth's Rivers	the three longest rivers	the Nile, the Amazon, and the Mississippi
10. U.S. Cities	the largest city	New York, New York
11. The Earth's Temperature	the highest recorded temperature	
12. The Earth's Surface	the equatorial diameter	

Note:
sq. mi. = square miles
mph = miles per hour
°F = degrees Fahrenheit

CHAPTER ASSIGNMENT: ASKING FOR INFORMATION

 Activity 5: Role Play

In Activity 5, you will use all of the language covered in Chapter Two: forming questions, introducing a topic, and thanking.

- Below you will find two student bio-data sheets. Your task is to work in groups of three to help these two fictitious students make important decisions.
- To do this, first read the bio-data sheets carefully. Then, formulate the questions you will use to get the information you need.
- Finally, go to the Student Housing Office, the Physical Education Department Office, and the Student Center that have been set up in the classroom and get the answers to the questions that you have formulated.
- When all students have returned to your group, complete your task by deciding what the two fictitious students should do. Be prepared to share your answers with the rest of the class.

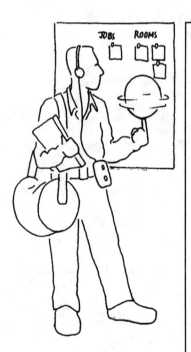

John Stoneman

John is a 20-year-old freshman. He's an engineering student from Newark, New Jersey. His hobbies are playing basketball, swimming, and listening to music. He is single.

John needs to decide the following:

- where to live
    - —He wants to live in the dorm if it is co-ed and it costs less than $4000/term.
    - —He prefers to eat in the dorm cafeteria, but he is a vegetarian.

- how to get regular exercise
    - —He wants to either go swimming or play tennis in the morning for one hour at least three times a week.

He also wants information about:

- any available part-time jobs on campus
- the nearest banking facilities
- when the bookstore is open

Sandra Crossman

Sandra is a 25-year-old freshman. She is a history major from Houston, Texas. She's married and has no children.

Sandra needs to decide the following:

- where to live
    —She wants to live in married student housing, but can pay only $4500 per term.
    —She is allergic to wheat and milk and would like to cook her own food.

- how to get regular exercise
    —Her first choice is to join a volleyball team, but she can only play in the mornings.
    —Her second choice is to play tennis, but she's not on the tennis team and doesn't have a racquet.

She also wants information about:

- parking a car on campus
- buying a university sweatshirt
- where the nearest place to mail a letter is

Activity 5: STUDENT A

STUDENT HOUSING OFFICE

ON-CAMPUS HOUSING

Dorm Information

Dorm	Type	Meals	Status
Adams Hall	Co-ed	Meals Included*	available
Cannon Hall	Co-ed	Meals not Included	full
Ingham Hall	Female	Meals Included*	available
Silson Hall	Male	Meals Included*	available
Toothill Hall	Married Students	N/A**	available

*Vegetarian meals available
**Not Applicable

Room Rates

Type	With Meals	Without Meals
Single	$3800	$2800
Double	$3300	$1800
Married	N/A	$4400

- Freshmen have priority in all cases except for married student housing, which is available on a first-come first-served basis.

- Rooms must be reserved for the **whole term**. No exceptions will be made.

OFF-CAMPUS HOUSING

This office has no information on off-campus housing. If you would like to live off campus, please consult a local newspaper.

Activity 5: STUDENT B

PHYSICAL EDUCATION DEPARTMENT OFFICE

SWIMMING
Pool Hours: Monday: 7:30 A.M.–8 P.M.
Tuesday: 7:30 A.M.–8 P.M.
Wednesday: Closed for swim team practice
Thursday: 7:30 A.M.–8 P.M.
Friday: 7:30 A.M.–8 P.M.
Saturday: Open to nonstudents
Sunday: Closed

VOLLEYBALL
The volleyball club meets every Monday,
Wednesday, and Friday.

Time: 6–8 P.M.
Place: Main Gym

TENNIS
Tennis courts reserved for class: Mon.–Fri., 9 A.M.–1 P.M.
Tennis courts are available for student use on weekdays from 1 P.M.
to sunset and all day on Saturdays, Sundays, and school holidays.
Reservations cannot be accepted.
Fees: Students: $1.00/hour — Nonstudents: $2.00/hour
(At least one player must be a student.)
Racquet Rental: $2.00/hour

Activity 5: STUDENT C

STUDENT CENTER

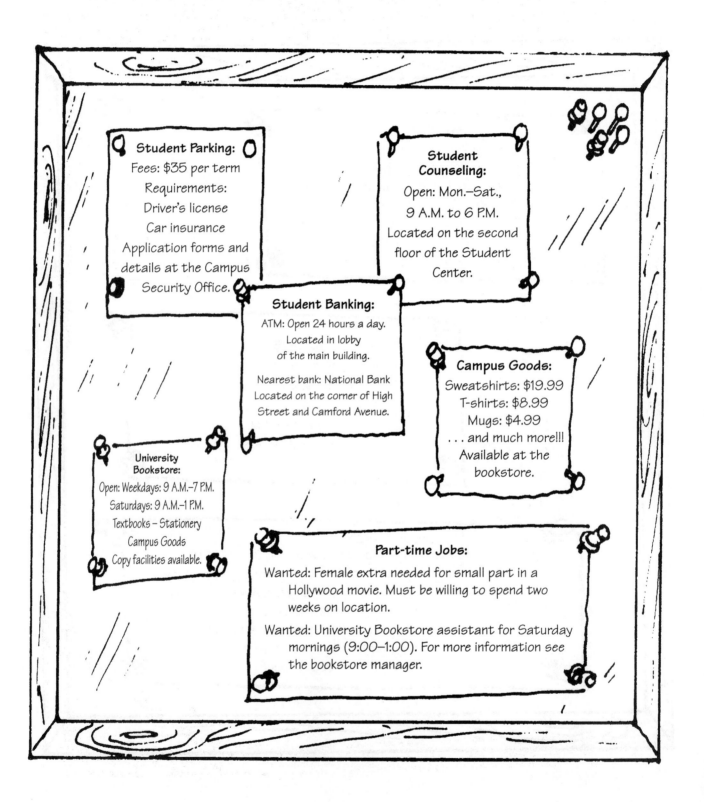

Student Parking:
Fees: $35 per term
Requirements:
Driver's license
Car insurance
Application forms and
details at the Campus
Security Office.

Student Counseling:
Open: Mon.–Sat.,
9 A.M. to 6 P.M.
Located on the second
floor of the Student
Center.

Student Banking:
ATM: Open 24 hours a day.
Located in lobby
of the main building.

Nearest bank: National Bank
Located on the corner of High
Street and Camford Avenue.

Campus Goods:
Sweatshirts: $19.99
T-shirts: $8.99
Mugs: $4.99
. . . and much more!!!
Available at the
bookstore.

University Bookstore:
Open: Weekdays: 9 A.M.–7 P.M.
Saturdays: 9 A.M.–1 P.M.
Textbooks – Stationery
Campus Goods
Copy facilities available.

Part-time Jobs:

Wanted: Female extra needed for small part in a
Hollywood movie. Must be willing to spend two
weeks on location.

Wanted: University Bookstore assistant for Saturday
mornings (9:00–1:00). For more information see
the bookstore manager.

CHAPTER TWO: *Summary of Key Language*

QUESTIONS

Yes–no questions

    Can I keep my pet cat in the dorm?

    Is there a bank on campus?

    Do you have any brochures on study abroad programs?

Wh- questions

    What time does the library open on Saturdays?

    How much does a parking permit cost?

    Where is the Psychology Department office?

INTRODUCING A TOPIC

I'd like some information on/about . . .

Do you have any information on/about . . .

Could you tell me about . . .

I'm interested in _____ . Do you have any information on that?

I was wondering if you had any information on/about . . .

I was wondering if you could tell me about . . .

THANKING

Thanks.

Thank you.

Thank you very much.

Thank you very much for your time.

Thank you. You've been very helpful.

Thank you for taking the time to talk with me. I really appreciate it.

Thanks anyway.

Thank you anyway.

OTHER

Chapter Three

Controlling a Conversation

INTRODUCTION

When speaking in English, it is important to remember that while it is the responsibility of the speaker to try to communicate a clear message, it is the responsibility of the listener to tell the speaker when he or she does not understand. For example, the listener may have to ask the speaker to speak more slowly or to repeat what has been said. These strategies for controlling a conversation are a normal part of native-speaker communication, and thus are necessary for non-native learners of English to master.

In Chapter Three, you will be introduced to and given opportunities to practice polite expressions for controlling a conversation.

Activity 1: Brainstorming

Working in pairs or groups of three, fill in these four boxes with as many expressions as you can think of.

Asking for a Definition

What does _____ mean?

Checking Spelling, Pronunciation, or Grammar

Could you spell that, please?

Asking for Repetition

Could you repeat that, please?

Confirming Meaning

Did you say . . . ?

DIALOGUE ANALYSIS

Listen to the dialogue one time for a general understanding.
Then listen again to complete Activity 2.

Situation: A teacher is giving an informal talk to a small group of students in his office.

Teacher:	Now, please feel free to interrupt me if there's anything you don't understand. I know that the topic of organic gardening is new to many of you, but it's important for us to study it because the increased use of chemicals in farming today concerns us all. Few people realize that the number of diseases caused by expo- ₅ sure to chemicals has increased exponentially in the last few years.
Student A:	Excuse me, but I'm not quite sure what you mean.
Teacher:	Well, what this basically means is that the number of people getting sick from chemicals is rising at a very high rate. ₁₀
Student A:	Ah, I see. Thank you.
Student B:	Excuse me, could you spell "exponentially" please?
Teacher:	Yes of course. It's E-X-P-O-N-E-N-T-I-A-L-L-Y.
Student B:	Thanks.
Teacher:	Now, in response to this, many people have started farming ₁₅ organically. The object of organic gardening is to grow plants without using chemical fertilizers or pesticides to control disease and pests. Organic gardeners use other kinds of controls, which can be divided into three types: cultural controls, physical controls, and biological controls. Chemical controls are used only as ₂₀ a last resort.
Student C:	I'm sorry, but could you repeat that last sentence please?
Teacher:	Yes. "Chemical controls are used only as a last resort."
Student C:	Thank you.
Teacher:	So, first of all, I would like to discuss cultural controls. Let's see ₂₅ . . . It's best to choose disease-resistant plants and important that you keep them healthy. Make sure the soil is fertile and make sure that it holds water. Use mulches to save water, control weeds, and add nutrients to the soil.

Student B:	I'm sorry. Could you explain what you mean by "mulches," 30 please?
Teacher:	Yes, mulch is a covering usually made from decaying plants, which is used to improve the soil and protect plant roots.
Student B:	I'm sorry. I didn't quite catch that. Could you repeat it, please?
Teacher:	Yes, mulch is made from decaying plants or other organic mate- 35 rials that are in the process of decomposing, and it is spread on the soil to improve the soil and to protect plant roots.
Student B:	Ah, I see.
Teacher:	You must also keep the garden clean. Don't plant any unhealthy plants. Wash all tools. Take out diseased plants or cut off dam- 40 aged areas. Plant your plants at the right time of year. Rotate crops to avoid soilborne disease.
Student A:	Excuse me, but what does "soilborne" mean?
Teacher:	A "soilborne disease" is one that comes from the soil itself as opposed to the air, for example. 45
Student C:	So are you saying that planting different crops at different times in the same soil will keep the soil healthier?
Teacher:	Exactly. Now, my final point under cultural controls is that companion planting can be used instead of chemicals. Companion planting, planting together plants that naturally ward off pests, 50 will repel pests.
Student B:	Could you give me an example of that?
Teacher:	Yes, of course. If you grow onions and carrots together, for example, you can ward off rust flies and some types of worms.
Student B:	That's very interesting. Thank you. 55
Teacher:	Now, with regard to the second and third categories, physical controls and biological controls . . .

 Activity 2: Highlighting and Categorizing

1. Highlight all of the expressions that the students use to *control the conversation*.
2. Add these eight expressions to the four categories listed in Activity 1.

PRACTICE 1: CHECKING INFORMATION

The purpose of Activity 3 is to practice checking information.

 Activity 3: Pairwork

STUDENT A

In this activity, you will practice asking questions about spelling, meaning, and parts of speech. On the next page is a grid that contains some words, their definitions, and their parts of speech. Your partner has a similar grid. Your task is to ask questions in order to fill in the missing spaces and to make sure that the existing words, definitions, and parts of speech are the **same** as those in your partner's grid.

- Ask what word your partner has in a particular box; for example, "What do you have in B4?"
- If you have nothing in the same box, fill it in with **all** the information that your partner has. Be sure to ask questions. Do not look at your partner's book.

If you have something in the same box, do the following:

- Check the spelling.
- Check whether the definition is the same.
- If anything is different, add it to your box.
- If the main word is **exactly** the same, write "Same."

- **Remember to use the key language given below and to check every box.**

Your partner will begin the activity by asking you what information you have in box A-1. Give only the information that is asked for. If neither you nor your partner knows how to pronounce a word, ask your teacher. After you have given your information for the first box, it is your turn to begin asking questions by saying:

Do you have anything in _____ ?
What (word) do you have in _____ ?

Key Language

Could you spell that, please?
How do you spell that?
What does _____ mean?
What part of speech is that?
Could you pronounce this word, please?
Could you repeat that, please?
Could you speak more slowly, please?

Activity 3: STUDENT A

	1	2	3	4
A	**matriculate:** to be accepted as a student at a university (verb)		**intonation:** the rise and fall in the level of the voice (noun)	
B		**regulation:** an official rule (noun)	**passed:** the past tense of the verb "to pass"	**seminar:** a small number of students working with a teacher on advanced study (noun)
C	**draft:** a partly written paper or plan (e.g., the early stages of an essay or speech) (noun)	**bibliography:** a list of books or articles (noun)		**anthology:** a collection of stories or poems (noun)
D		**site:** a location (noun)	**board:** a flat piece of material, often wood; a blackboard (noun)	**research:** advanced study of a subject to learn more about it (noun)

PRACTICE 1: CHECKING INFORMATION

The purpose of Activity 3 is to practice checking information.

 Activity 3: Pairwork

STUDENT B

In this activity, you will practice asking questions about spelling, meaning, and parts of speech. On the next page is a grid that contains some words, their definitions, and their parts of speech. Your partner has a similar grid. Your task is to ask questions in order to fill in the missing spaces and to make sure that the existing words, definitions, and parts of speech are the **same** as those in your partner's grid.

- Ask what word your partner has in a particular box; for example, "What do you have in B4?"
- If you have nothing in the same box, fill it in with **all** the information that your partner has. Be sure to ask questions. Do not look at your partner's book.

If you have something in the same box, do the following:

- Check the spelling.
- Check whether the definition is the same.
- If anything is different, add it to your box.
- If the main word is **exactly** the same, write "Same."

- **Remember to use the key language given below and to check every box.**

Then, ask more questions to get enough information to fill in the box. If neither you nor your partner knows how to pronounce a word, ask your teacher. When you have filled in the box, it is your partner's turn to ask for information. Give only the information that is asked for. Ask questions by saying things like:

Do you have anything in _____ ?
What (word) do you have in _____ ?

Key Language

> Could you spell that, please?
> How do you spell that?
> What does _____ mean?
> What part of speech is that?
> Could you pronounce this word, please?
> Could you repeat that, please?
> Could you speak more slowly, please?

Activity 3: STUDENT B

	1	2	3	4
A		**illegible:** something that cannot be read, unreadable (adjective)		**plagiarize:** to use someone else's words or ideas without admitting it (verb)
B	**periodical:** a magazine or journal that appears regularly (noun)	**regulation:** an official rule (noun)	**past:** earlier than the present (noun)	
C	**draught:** taking liquid, such as beer, from a barrel (noun)		**paraphrase:** to say something in a different way that is usually easier to understand (verb)	**anthology:** a collection of stories or poems (noun)
D	**delete:** to remove or erase, usually words (verb)	**cite:** to quote (verb)	**bored:** uninterested (adjective)	

PRACTICE 2: SEEKING CLARIFICATION

The purpose of Activity 4 is to practice using the language for asking for repetition, checking spelling, and asking for a definition.

 Activity 4: Pairwork Dictation

STUDENT A

On the facing page you will find a short passage called "Getting the Information You Need," and a space for writing. Your partner has the second part of the passage called "Performing a Balancing Act." Together, the two passages will give you some important information. Your task is to dictate the information to each other so that both of you have all the information.

- Begin the activity by reading your passage to your partner at normal speed. Do not slow down unless your partner asks you to do so. Do not repeat, spell a word, or provide a definition unless asked to do so. Some words in the passage are written in **bold**; they are defined at the bottom of the page.
- When you have finished, your partner will read the second passage. Write down **exactly** what is said. Your partner will not repeat or give any information unless you ask.
- **Remember to use the key language given at the bottom of this page.**
- When you have both finished, compare your passages and make any necessary corrections.
- Count the number of corrections and report them to your teacher.
- The pair with the least number of corrections wins the game!

Key Language

Asking for a Definition	*Checking Spelling, Pronunciation, or Grammar*
What does ___ mean?	Could you spell that, please?
Excuse me, what is the meaning of ___ ?	Could you pronounce this word, please?
I'm not sure what you mean.	How do you spell that?
I'm sorry, but I don't understand what you mean.	How do you pronounce this word?
Could you explain what you mean by ___ ?	What part of speech is that?
Could you give me an example?	
Asking for Repetition	*Paraphrasing to Confirm Meaning*
Could you repeat that, please?	Did you say . . . ?
Excuse me, could you please repeat that from the beginning?	Do you mean . . . ?
Pardon me, could you please repeat the last sentence?	Are you saying that . . . ?
Could you speak more slowly, please?	

Activity 4: STUDENT A

Part One—Getting the Information You Need

In order to **flourish** in an English-speaking environment, students of English need to find ways of getting information. One way to ensure that they **comprehend** everything that is being said is for them to learn to stop a speaker and ask her to repeat, spell, or provide additional information. Because many students of English may be **reluctant** to interrupt a speaker, it is **imperative** that all students learn and practice the expressions that are commonly used for this purpose. Through **dedicated** practice all students can gain confidence and control, making the most of every encounter they have with an English speaker.

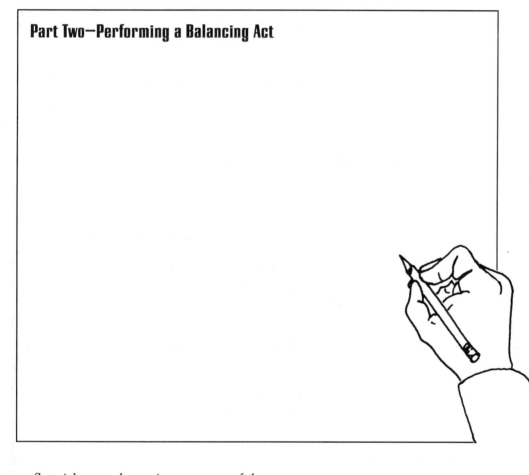

Part Two—Performing a Balancing Act

to flourish — to be active or successful
to comprehend — to understand
to be reluctant — to be hesitant or unwilling
imperative — necessary
dedicated — committed, very interested in, or working very hard for

PRACTICE 2: SEEKING CLARIFICATION

The purpose of Activity 4 is to practice using the language for asking for repetition, checking spelling, and asking for a definition.

Activity 4: Pairwork Dictation

STUDENT B

On the facing page you will find a short passage called "Performing a Balancing Act," and a space for writing. Your partner has the first part of the passage called "Getting the Information You Need." Together, the two passages will give you some important information. Your task is to dictate the information to each other so that both of you have all the information.

- Your partner will begin the activity by reading his or her passage. Write down **exactly** what is said. Your partner will not repeat or give any information unless you ask.
- **Remember to use the key language listed at the bottom of this page.**
- When your partner has finished, read your passage to your partner at normal speed. Do not slow down unless your partner asks you to do so. Do not repeat, spell a word, or provide a definition unless asked to do so. Some words in the passage are written in **bold**; they are defined at the bottom of the page.
- When both of you have finished, compare your passages and make any necessary corrections.
- Count the number of corrections and report them to your teacher.
- The pair with the least number of corrections wins the game!

Key Language

Asking for a Definition	*Checking Spelling, Pronunciation, or Grammar*
What does ___ mean?	Could you spell that, please?
Excuse me, what is the meaning of ___ ?	Could you pronounce this word, please?
I'm not sure what you mean.	How do you spell that?
I'm sorry, but I don't understand what you mean.	How do you pronounce this word?
Could you explain what you mean by ___ ?	What part of speech is that?
Could you give me an example?	
Asking for Repetition	*Paraphrasing to Confirm Meaning*
Could you repeat that, please?	Did you say . . . ?
Excuse me, could you please repeat that from the beginning?	Do you mean . . . ?
Pardon me, could you please repeat the last sentence?	Are you saying that . . . ?
Could you speak more slowly, please?	

Activity 4: STUDENT B

Part One—Getting the Information You Need

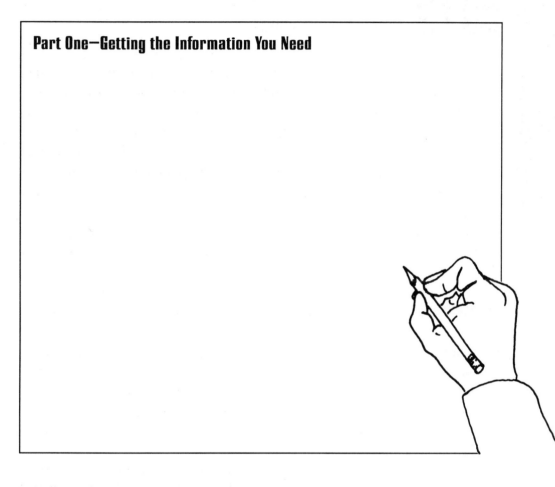

Part Two—Performing a Balancing Act

It should also be mentioned that some students, particularly those who are somewhat more **loquacious** than others, may have to hold their tongues once in a while rather than interrupting the speaker at every opportunity that presents itself. Indeed, it is important **to assert** oneself, but it is also **crucial** that one respect the speaker, especially one who **outranks** you. Similarly, students who are overly **reticent** to speak up in public may need to push themselves to stop a speaker when necessary. Otherwise, they may find themselves at the end of a conversational exchange and suddenly realize that they just haven't understood at all.

loquacious — talkative
to assert — to act in a way that shows one's power or control
crucial — very important
to outrank — to rank above, to be more respected
reticent — reserved, quiet, silent

CHAPTER ASSIGNMENT: CONTROLLING A CONVERSATION

 Activity 5: Storytelling

In Activity 5, you will practice using all of the language we have learned in this chapter. Work in groups of four, with each group member using a different worksheet. Each worksheet contains two sections: one part of a four-part story, and a list of difficult words that can be found in one of the other three sections. Your group's task is to help each other understand the whole story **without** reading your section aloud and **without** looking at each other's worksheets.

If you succeed in your task, then you should be able to answer the questions on page 53. But you **must not look** at the questions until your group is sure that everyone understands the whole story.

Procedure

* Read your section of the story and underline any words you don't understand.
* Ask the other members of your group about these unfamiliar words. Use the vocabulary list at the bottom of your worksheet to answer the other students' vocabulary questions. Remember to use the key language when asking for definitions.
* When all members of your group understand their part of the story, Student A begins telling the story without looking at the worksheet. You do not need to memorize the story word for word. Paraphrase, but be sure to include all the information. When Student A has finished, Students B, C, and D continue telling the story in order.

* Ask about anything you don't understand, using the language you have learned in this chapter for controlling a conversation.

When your group is sure that everyone understands the story, turn to page 53 and answer the questions.

Activity 5: STUDENT A

Two hunters got up very early one morning, looked out of their tent at the darkening sky and knew that their task was going to be a formidable one. They had decided the night before that on this particular day they would go hunting for bears, and while the idea excited them, the potential dangers left them feeling vulnerable. They ate breakfast in a rather somber mood and when they had finished, they packed their bags with the day's provisions, picked up their rifles, and started their trek south. It was eight o'clock exactly.

Vocabulary

trudging (to trudge) = v. to walk heavily
motionless = adj. without moving
to drag = v. to pull along
a culprit = n. a guilty person
ensued (to ensue) = v. happened
majestic = adj. great, powerful
in unison = n. together, at the same time

Notepad

Activity 5: STUDENT B

They had gone south for a mile, silently trudging along side by side, when the shorter one stopped, turned to the other and suggested in her inimitable way, that their hopes of finding a bear in this direction were rather forlorn. Once again silence ensued, but a few seconds later they turned in unison and headed toward the east. They had gone half a mile when they both came to an abrupt halt. About a quarter of a mile in front of them stood the biggest, most majestic looking bear either of them had ever seen. Even at this distance his power and ferocity could be clearly seen.

Vocabulary

vulnerable = adj. easily harmed, hurt, or attacked
to creep = v. to move slowly and quietly
laborious = adj. needing great effort
somber = adj. sad
a trigger = n. the part of a gun that is pushed when firing
a conquest = n. something taken by force
potential = adj. possible

Notepad

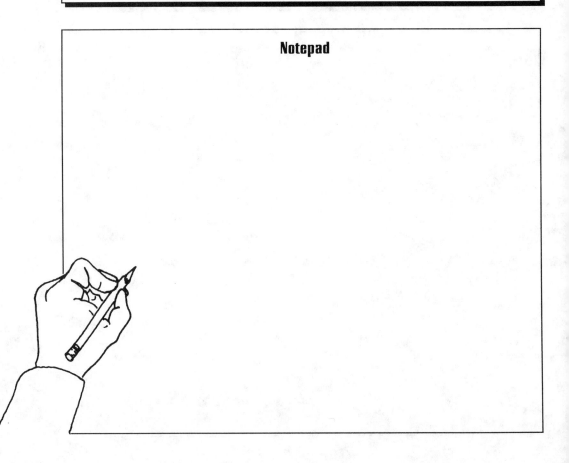

Activity 5: STUDENT C

Luckily the bear had not seen them, so very quietly and with no sudden movements, they began to creep toward the bear. The bear remained motionless, his coat gleaming in the mid-morning sun. The taller of the two hunters meticulously took out her rifle and was just about to pull the trigger when the bear suddenly caught sight of them and began to run off toward the east. The two hunters gave chase and exactly half a mile from where they had originally stood and watched him, the taller hunter shot and killed the bear with a lone bullet to the head.

Vocabulary

formidable = adj. difficult
provisions = n. food and other supplies
forlorn = adj. hopeless
amiss = adj. wrong
onerous = adj. difficult, troublesome
ferocity = n. meanness, violence, wildness
halt = n. stop

Notepad

Activity 5: STUDENT D

The two hunters were delighted with their conquest, but now came the onerous task of transporting the bear back to their camp. They had no choice but to drag him, so walking the mile north back to their camp was a slow and laborious journey. After almost two hours, they finally came within sight of the camp, but as they drew nearer, they both realized there was something terribly amiss. In their absence, their camp had been completely destroyed, and from the footprints they knew that the culprit was another bear!

Vocabulary

gleaming = adj. shining
trek = n. journey, hike
abrupt = adj. sudden
meticulously = adv. carefully
lone = adj. single
inimitable = adj. too good for anyone else to copy

Notepad

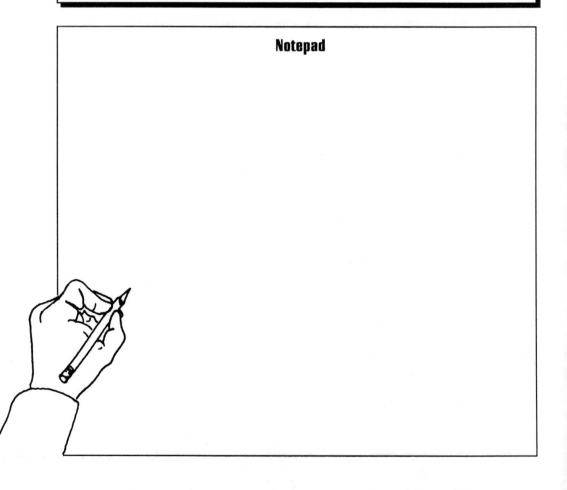

Activity 5: Storytelling Worksheet

The sections of the story you have just read contain enough information to answer four of the five questions below. Discuss them as a group and if you are sure of your answers write them in the space below and send one student to the teacher to check if your answers are correct. For the **one** question that is impossible to answer, just write "Don't know."

If you cannot answer four of the five questions below, go back and check your section of the story again. Then discuss the story as a group and try to work out the answers you are not sure of. When you think you know them, write them in the space below and ask your teacher to check them.

If your teacher tells you some of the answers are wrong, follow the instructions in the paragraph above!

QUESTIONS	ANSWERS
1. How many bears were in the story?	
2. How many shots were fired?	
3. What was the color of the bear that destroyed their camp?	
4. How many men were in the story?	
5. How much time passes in the story?	

CHAPTER THREE: *Summary of Key Language*

ASKING FOR A DEFINITION

What does _____ mean?

Excuse me, what is the meaning of _____ ?

I'm not sure what you mean.

I'm sorry, but I don't understand what you mean.

Could you explain what you mean by _____ ?

Could you give me an example?

CHECKING SPELLING, PRONUNCIATION, OR GRAMMAR

Could you spell that, please?

Could you pronounce this word, please?

How do you spell that?

How do you pronounce this word?

What part of speech is that?

ASKING FOR REPETITION

Could you repeat that, please?

Excuse me, could you please repeat that from the beginning?

Pardon me, could you please repeat the last sentence?

Could you speak more slowly, please?

PARAPHRASING TO CONFIRM MEANING

Did you say . . . ?

Do you mean . . . ?

Are you saying that . . . ?

OTHER

Chapter Four

Active Listening Skills

INTRODUCTION

In English conversations the listener is expected to play an active role by giving both verbal and nonverbal feedback to the speaker. An active listener lets the speaker know that the listener is interested in what the speaker is saying. This encourages the speaker to continue and helps build a bond between the speaker and the listener.

In Chapter Four, you will learn how to be a more active listener, a useful skill not only in academic situations, but also in everyday conversations.

 Activity 1: Brainstorming

1. Make a list of the nonverbal signs that active listeners use to show that they are paying attention.
2. What sounds, such as "uh-huh," have you heard native speakers of English use to show that they are listening actively?
3. In what other ways do listeners show that they are paying attention?
4. In what ways do listeners show that they are not paying attention or want to end the conversation?

DIALOGUE ANALYSIS

 ### Activity 2: Listening and Classifying Verbal Feedback

Listen to the dialogue and, using the chart below, count the number of times the husband makes the following responses:

Tag Responses:	
Sounds:	
Wh- questions:	

Once you have listened to the dialogue, read it over and check your answers to Activity 2.

Situation: A husband and wife are at home when a man knocks at the door.

(Knock, Knock)

Agent:	Good afternoon.	
Husband:	Good afternoon.	
Agent:	I'm looking for a Mr. Wright.	
Husband:	Are you? (nodding)	
Agent:	Mr. Ernest Wright?	5
Husband:	Uh huh. (smiling)	
Agent:	Mr. Ernest B. Wright?	
Husband:	Mmm. (nodding and smiling) **What do you want?**	
Agent:	Well, it's about the money.	
Husband:	Is it?	10
Agent:	The money from the lottery.	
Husband:	Oh, really? (nodding, smiling, eyes wide open)	
Agent:	I'm the agent in charge of winning tickets.	
Husband:	Are you? (nodding very slowly, eyes getting wider)	
Agent:	Your name is E. B. Wright, isn't it?	15
Husband:	Mmm. (still nodding slowly)	
Agent:	Well you've just won $1000. Your wife telephoned earlier with the winning combination.	
Husband:	Did she? (smiling broadly and looking directly at the agent)	
Agent:	Just sign here.	20
Husband:	Can I sign with my left hand? I hurt my right hand yesterday.	
Agent:	Yes, of course. Here's your money.	

Husband:	Thank you. (still smiling broadly, but looking directly at the money)
Agent:	Congratulations Mr. Wright. Good-bye. 25
Husband:	Good-bye. (He closes the door and goes inside.)
Wife:	Who was that, dear?
Husband:	Someone looking for Ernest Wright.
Wife:	Did you tell him he lives next door? 30
Husband:	Mmm. (smiling very broadly and putting the money in his pocket)

 Activity 3: Pairwork

Nonverbal Feedback

- Work in pairs. One partner will give information about one of the following topics:
    - his or her family
    - his or her country (if you are from different countries) or his or her hometown
    - his or her favorite sport
- The other partner will listen actively, and respond **nonverbally** by nodding, smiling, making eye contact, and writing down three interesting pieces of information.
- Keep talking until your teacher tells you to stop.
- Switch roles and begin again.
- Check with your partner and give feedback about whether or not you both used nonverbal feedback effectively.

Verbal Feedback

- Now you are going to talk about the same topic with a different partner.
- This time, however, your partner will add **verbal** feedback, for example,

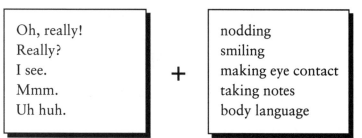

Oh, really! Really? I see. Mmm. Uh huh.	nodding smiling making eye contact taking notes body language

(with a **+** between the two boxes)

- Switch roles when your teacher tells you to, and remember to take notes as you did earlier.

PRACTICE 1: GIVING VERBAL AND NONVERBAL FEEDBACK

The purpose of Activity 3 is to practice using verbal and nonverbal feedback to show that you are listening actively.

Activity 4: Fluency Circles

- Choose and complete six of the partial sentences provided below.
- Your teacher will ask the class to form two circles, one inside the other.
- When you are told to begin, the students on the outside circle should say each of the sentences on their lists to the student facing them on the inside circle.
- After each sentence, their partners should respond with an appropriate tag response.
- See how fast you can make six correct tag responses.
- Switch roles.
- When all pairs have finished, your teacher will ask the students on the outside circle to rotate one place.
- Repeat the activity, switching roles.

Partial Sentences

I am _____ .

I like _____ .

I have been _____ .

I will _____ .

My father is _____ .

My mother has _____ .

My sister was _____ .

I was _____ .

My dog _____ .

My room _____ .

My brother has never _____ .

My parents are _____ .

Sample Tag Responses

Student A:	I've been to the Grand Canyon five times!
Student B:	**Have you?**
Student A:	Yes. It's a beautiful place.
Student A:	My favorite color is blue.
Student B:	**Is it?**
Student A:	Yes.

Activity 5: Storytelling

In this activity, you are going to work in groups of four, telling a number of group stories. The stories will have four rounds. In every round each student will either make up a part of the story or ask a wh- question to help the story continue.

PRACTICE 3: USING WH- QUESTIONS

The purpose of Activity 5 is to practice using wh- questions to listen actively.

- Sit in a circle with the other three members of your group.
- Your teacher will give you some strips of paper. Each strip contains the first line of a story. Leave them face down on the desk.
- When your teacher tells you to begin, Student A picks up a strip of paper from the desk and reads the first line of the story to the rest of the group.
- Student B then makes up the second line of the story.
- Student C adds the next line of the story.
- Student D asks a wh- question.
- Then the next round begins with Student A making up the next line of the story by answering Student D's question.
- In this round Student C asks the question, then in the next round Student B, and in the final round Student A.
- At the end of the fourth round, the last person to speak should try to finish off the story.
- The next story begins with student B picking up a strip of paper and reading it to the group.
- The activity ends when all of the strips of paper have been used.
- Before you begin, practice reading the sample dialogue on the next page with your group members.

Activity 5: Sample Dialogue

Round 1:	Student A:	(Reads.) **It was an unusually cold winter . . .**
	Student B:	. . . and the water pipes in our house froze.
	Student C:	So, we decided to go on a ski vacation.
	Student D:	**Where did you go?**
Round 2:	Student A:	We went to Vermont because we had heard it was a great place to ski.
	Student B:	But my mother had never learned to ski!
	Student C:	**So, what did she do?**
	Student D:	Well, she decided that if her husband and her three children could ski, then she would also learn.
Round 3:	Student A:	So, at five o'clock the next morning she secretly got up, borrowed my father's skis and went out to practice by herself.
	Student B:	**What happened next?**
	Student C:	Well, it took her nearly an hour to get to the top of the beginner's slope because the ski lift wasn't open and the skis were heavy.
	Student D:	Then she set off skiing and falling down the slope.
Round 4:	Student A:	**What was the rest of her family doing?**
	Student B:	Well, when we got up and found her gone we started looking for her. We looked inside the hotel and our father went to look around outside.
	Student C:	He looked across at the slopes and saw his wife skiing. She kept falling, but he was still very proud of her for trying by herself.
	Student D:	So, he walked over to meet her, to congratulate her. But as he got nearer, she speeded up, lost all control and crashed into my father! He ended up with a broken arm, and my mother spent the rest of the vacation taking care of him. She never went skiing again!

Wh- questions
Who . . . What . . . Where . . . When . . . Why . . . How . . . ?

CHAPTER ASSIGNMENT: BEING AN ACTIVE LISTENER

Activity 6: Role Play

- For this activity you will work in groups of four.
- Two students will speak while the other two students evaluate each of the speakers, using the Active Listening Skills Evaluation Form on the next page. (Make sure that the two evaluators are not evaluating the same speaker!)
- Your goal is to role play the situation below, continuing the conversation for at least ten minutes. **Make sure that both speakers participate equally.**
- **Remember to use both nonverbal and verbal active listening skills.**
- Have fun and be creative!
- Change roles after the first two students have spoken for ten minutes.

Situation: Two students from the same English class run into each other in the cafeteria and decide to have lunch together. They start to discuss some of the topics below, using the active listening skills that they have just finished studying in their English class.

- The campus
- School life
- Your classes
- Homework
- The friends you've made
- Your English ability

- Your dorm/housing
- The cafeteria food
- The sports facilities
- The student union or student center
- The library
- The area around campus

Activity 6: Evaluation Form

Active Listening Skills—Evaluation Form

Name of Speaker: _____

Name of Evaluator: _____

Your role as the evaluator is to watch the speakers and listen carefully to what they are saying, and to fill in this evaluation form for one of the speakers by putting a ✓ next to each expression used.

Start Time: _____

I. Nonverbal Feedback: **COMMENTS:**

eye contact   _____
nodding   _____
smiling   _____

Other?   _____

II. Verbal Feedback:

Oh, really!   _____
Really?   _____
I see.   _____
Mmm.   _____
Uh huh.   _____

Other?   _____

III. Tag Responses:_____

IV. Wh- questions:_____

End Time: _____

Speaking Time: (Circle one)   0% — 20% — 40% — 50% — 60% — 80% — 100%

CHAPTER FOUR: *Summary of Key Language*

Since the focus of this chapter is on active listening skills, the key language for this chapter is not as substantial as for other chapters. However, the following will serve as a reminder of the material covered.

VERBAL FEEDBACK

Oh, really?

Really?

I see.

Mmm.

Uh huh.

NONVERBAL FEEDBACK

Nodding

Smiling

Eye contact

Note-taking

Body language

TAG RESPONSES

Did she?

Are you?

Were they?

Has she?

Will he?

WH- QUESTIONS

Who . . . ?

What . . . ?

Where . . . ?

When . . . ?

Why . . . ?

How . . . ?

OTHER

UNIT ASSIGNMENT: GETTING INFORMATION ON CAMPUS

This activity is an excellent opportunity for your group to go out onto campus to find answers to any questions you may still have about your institution and campus life. To begin, choose four places from the list below, one for each member of your group. Next, using the worksheet on the following page, brainstorm questions you could ask in order to get information that you would like to know. For homework, go individually to these places and ask the questions you have formulated. Don't forget to be an active listener and to use all of the skills that you have learned for asking for information and controlling a conversation. When you return to class, your group will meet again to share the information that you have gathered.

- The Library
- The Student Union (The Student Center)
- The Physical Education Department
- Campus Security
- The Housing Office
- The Career Center
- The Health Center
- The Student Advising Center
- University Department Offices (e.g., the History Dept., English Dept., etc.)
- The Financial Aid Office
- The Bookstore
- The Tutoring Center
- The Dean of Students Office
- Other?

After you have presented your information to the group, together discuss your information-gathering experiences:

1. What was most satisfying about your experience? (Were you able to understand what was being said? Did you find that you were able to control the conversation well? Did you get some unexpected/useful/surprising information?)

2. What difficulties did you encounter while getting information?

3. What will you do differently next time?

Campus Information Worksheet

Place visited: _____

Name of person(s) asked: _____

Job Title(s): _____

Questions to be asked:

Information obtained:

UNIT 3
The Teacher's Office

UNIT OUTLINE

Chapter Five: **MAKING AN APPOINTMENT**

>   Introduction
>   Dialogue Analysis
>   Practice: Negotiating a Time
>   Chapter Assignment: Making an Appointment
>   Summary of Key Language

Chapter Six: **VISITING A TEACHER'S OFFICE**

>   Introduction
>   Dialogue Analysis
>   Practice 1: Opening a Conversation, Stating One's
>   Business, and Closing a Conversation
>   Practice 2: Providing Explanations
>   Practice 3: Knowing When It's Time to Leave
>   Chapter Assignment: Visiting a Teacher's Office
>   Summary of Key Language

UNIT ASSIGNMENT: Visiting a Teacher's Office

Chapter Five

Making an Appointment

INTRODUCTION

For many students, the quality of their education depends not only on the relationships that they form with other students, but also on the rapport that they establish with their teachers. One way that teachers make themselves available to students outside of class is by holding regular office hours. They may announce their office hours during the first week of class or post an office hour schedule on or near their office door. Though most teachers encourage students to drop in at any time during their regular office hours, making an appointment is generally recommended as it is considered more courteous and because students with appointments are often given priority.

Many teachers are also available at other times for students who have urgent questions or cannot meet during office hours, but it is best to make an appointment so that your teacher will be available for you at a particular time. This first chapter of Unit 3 focuses on how to make an appointment.

 Activity 1: Pairwork

Discuss the following with your partner.

1. Have you ever made an appointment to see a teacher? If so, what was the reason? If not, why not?
2. What are all the reasons you can think of for visiting a teacher's office?
3. Please circle any of the following words that describe your feelings about visiting a teacher's office and explain to your partner why you feel this way.

excited	scared	worried	interested
terrified	comfortable	uncertain	shy

DIALOGUE ANALYSIS

 Activity 2: Gap-Filling

Listen to the dialogue carefully for a general understanding of the conversation. Then listen again and fill in the missing information below. Compare your answers with your partner's and listen a third time, if necessary.

Situation: Patricia has come to her teacher's office to ask him some questions about her essay. However, Mr. Mills is busy, so she makes an appointment to see him later.

(Knock, Knock)

Mr. Mills: Come in.

Patricia: _____ ?
(1 - OPENING A CONVERSATION)

Mr. Mills: Well, I'm afraid I'm on my way to a meeting. What would you like to talk about?

Patricia: I'd like to ask you a few questions about the essay assignment. 5

_____ ?
(2 - MAKING AN APPOINTMENT)

Mr. Mills: Sure. I'll be free after lunch, but I have a class at 2:30.

_____ ?
(3 - NEGOTIATING A TIME)

Patricia: Mmm . . . I have a class at 2:30 too._____ 1:30?
(4 - NEGOTIATING A TIME)

Mr. Mills: Well, actually, I have another student coming to see me at that 10

time. _____ 1:45?
(5 - NEGOTIATING A TIME)

Patricia: Yes. That would be fine with me.

Mr. Mills: Good, then I'll see you at 1:45.

Patricia: Okay._____. Bye.
(6 - CLOSING A CONVERSATION)

Mr. Mills: Bye. 15

Activity 3: Bingo Mingle

Your task is to make appointments with other students and to complete one line of the schedule below. The line can be vertical, horizontal, or a five-space diagonal. The first student to complete a line shouts "BINGO!"

- Your teacher will give you a list of days and times.

- *When asking for the appointment,* you can ask for any time that is free on your schedule.

- *When agreeing to an appointment,* you can agree only to the times on your list.

- After you agree on a time, both students should put the appointment on their schedules by writing the other person's name in the appropriate space below.

- You may write the name of each student you meet twice: once when you ask for an appointment, and once when you agree to an appointment.

- When you have entered a name, begin a conversation with another student.

PRACTICE: NEGOTIATING A TIME

The purpose of this activity is to practice negotiating a time, using the key language discussed in this chapter. To begin, practice the dialogue below in pairs, paying special attention to the key language.

Sample Dialogue

Andrew:	I'd like to make an appointment to see you.
Brenda:	Okay. What time would be convenient for you?
Andrew:	How about Wednesday at 4:00?
Brenda:	I'm sorry, but I'm busy at that time.
Andrew:	Okay. Are you free at 2:00 on Tuesday?
Brenda:	Yes, that's fine.

	Monday	*Tuesday*	*Wednesday*	*Thursday*	*Friday*
1:00					
2:00					
3:00					
4:00					
5:00					

CHAPTER ASSIGNMENT: MAKING AN APPOINTMENT

Activity 4: Role Play   STUDENT A

Activity 4 consists of three role plays. In the first role play you will play a student, in the second you will play a teacher, and in the third you will be the evaluator. Try to do the role plays without looking at the key language on the right side of the page. If you finish before the other groups, you may switch role sheets and begin again.

ROLE ONE: STUDENT

You are a student. You would like to make an appointment to see your teacher to discuss today's homework assignment. You are free this afternoon from 1:00 to 2:00 and from 3:00 to 3:30. Tomorrow morning you are free from 11:00 to 12:00. Arrange a time to meet with your teacher. • Remember to use the appropriate expressions for making an appointment.	**KEY LANGUAGE:** *Opening a conversation* "Excuse me, but do you have a minute?" *Making an appointment* "I'd like to make an appointment to . . . " "Could I make an appointment to . . . ?" *Negotiating a time* "What time would be convenient for you?" "Are you free at . . . ?" "How about . . . ?" "What about . . . ?" "I'm sorry, but I'm busy at that time." "Yes, that's fine." *Closing a conversation* "Thank you very much. I'll see you then."

ROLE TWO: TEACHER

You are a teacher. You are busy all afternoon today, but you are free all day tomorrow.	**KEY LANGUAGE:** *Negotiating a time* "What time would be convenient for you?" "Are you free at . . . ?" "How about . . . ?" "What about . . . ?" "I'm sorry, but I'm busy at that time." "Yes, that's fine."

ROLE THREE: EVALUATOR

You are the evaluator. Using the speaker evaluation form on page 75, evaluate the member of your group who is playing the role of the **student**. After the role play is finished, quickly discuss the results of the evaluation with that student.	

CHAPTER ASSIGNMENT: MAKING AN APPOINTMENT

Activity 4: Role Play   STUDENT B

Activity 4 consists of three role plays. In the first role play you will play a teacher, in the second you will be the evaluator, and in the third you will play a student. Try to do the role plays without looking at the key language on the right side of the page. If you finish before the other groups, you may switch role sheets and begin again.

ROLE ONE: TEACHER	
You are a teacher. You would be happy to talk with this student, but you are busy all afternoon. You can see the student anytime tomorrow morning.	**KEY LANGUAGE:** *Negotiating a time* "What time would be convenient for you?" "Are you free at . . . ?" "How about . . . ?" "What about . . . ?" "I'm sorry, but I'm busy at that time." "Yes, that's fine."

ROLE TWO: EVALUATOR	
You are the evaluator. Using the speaker evaluation form on page 75, evaluate the member of your group who is playing the role of the **student**. After the role play is finished, quickly discuss the results of the evaluation with that student.	

ROLE THREE: STUDENT	
You are a student. You would like to make an appointment with your teacher to discuss the organization of your essay. You are free all afternoon today and tomorrow afternoon from 3:00 to 5:00. Make an appointment for a time when you are both available. • Remember to use the appropriate expressions for making an appointment.	**KEY LANGUAGE:** *Opening a conversation* "Excuse me, but do you have a minute?" *Making an appointment* "I'd like to make an appointment to . . . " "Could I make an appointment to . . . ?" *Negotiating a time* "What time would be convenient for you?" "Are you free at . . . ?" "How about . . . ?" "What about . . . ?" "I'm sorry, but I'm busy at that time." "Yes, that's fine." *Closing a conversation* "Thank you very much. I'll see you then."

CHAPTER ASSIGNMENT: MAKING AN APPOINTMENT

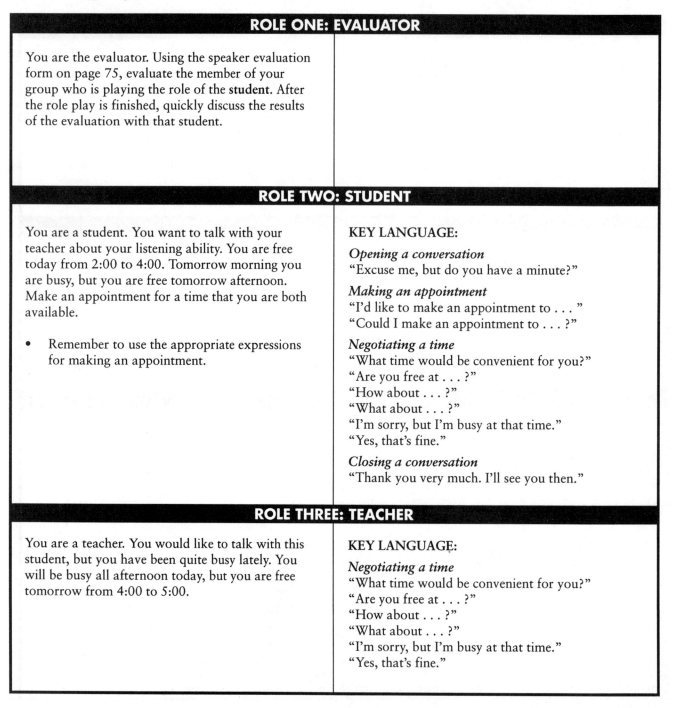

Activity 4: Role Play   STUDENT C

Activity 4 consists of three role plays. In the first role play you will be the evaluator, in the second you will play a student, and in the third you will play a teacher. Try to do the role plays without looking at the key language on the right side of the page. If you finish before the other groups, you may switch role sheets and begin again.

ROLE ONE: EVALUATOR

You are the evaluator. Using the speaker evaluation form on page 75, evaluate the member of your group who is playing the role of the **student**. After the role play is finished, quickly discuss the results of the evaluation with that student.

ROLE TWO: STUDENT

You are a student. You want to talk with your teacher about your listening ability. You are free today from 2:00 to 4:00. Tomorrow morning you are busy, but you are free tomorrow afternoon. Make an appointment for a time that you are both available.

- Remember to use the appropriate expressions for making an appointment.

KEY LANGUAGE:

Opening a conversation
"Excuse me, but do you have a minute?"

Making an appointment
"I'd like to make an appointment to . . . "
"Could I make an appointment to . . . ?"

Negotiating a time
"What time would be convenient for you?"
"Are you free at . . . ?"
"How about . . . ?"
"What about . . . ?"
"I'm sorry, but I'm busy at that time."
"Yes, that's fine."

Closing a conversation
"Thank you very much. I'll see you then."

ROLE THREE: TEACHER

You are a teacher. You would like to talk with this student, but you have been quite busy lately. You will be busy all afternoon today, but you are free tomorrow from 4:00 to 5:00.

KEY LANGUAGE:

Negotiating a time
"What time would be convenient for you?"
"Are you free at . . . ?"
"How about . . . ?"
"What about . . . ?"
"I'm sorry, but I'm busy at that time."
"Yes, that's fine."

Activity 4: Evaluation Form

Making An Appointment: Speaker Evaluation Form

Evaluator: _____   *Student Role:* _____

As the evaluator, your task is to listen carefully to the other two students in your group and to put a ✓ next to the expressions used by the person who is playing the role of the student. Also, try to add some comments about performance. For example, what active listening skills did he or she use well? Was the student able to communicate his or her ideas clearly? Was his or her pronunciation clear and easy to understand? During your discussion with the person you evaluated, be sure to comment on whether that student remembered to do each of the following:

Opening a conversation

_____ "Excuse me, but do you have a minute?"

Making an appointment

_____ "I'd like to make an appointment to . . . "
_____ "Could I make an appointment to . . . ?"

Negotiating a time

_____ "What time would be convenient for you?"
_____ "Are you free at . . . ?"
_____ "How about . . . ?"
_____ "What about . . . ?"
_____ "I'm sorry, but I'm busy at that time."
_____ "Yes, that's fine."

Closing a conversation

_____ "Thank you very much. I'll see you then."

Comments:

CHAPTER FIVE: *Summary of Key Language*

OPENING A CONVERSATION

Excuse me, but do you have a minute?

MAKING AN APPOINTMENT

I'd like to make an appointment to see you.

I'd like to make an appointment to discuss . . .

Could I make an appointment to talk about . . . ?

Could I make an appointment to see you?

NEGOTIATING A TIME

What time would be convenient for you?

Are you free at . . . ?

How about . . . ?

What about . . . ?

I'm sorry, but I'm busy at that time.

Yes, that's fine.

CLOSING A CONVERSATION

Thank you very much. I'll see you then.

OTHER

Chapter Six

Visiting a Teacher's Office

INTRODUCTION

As mentioned in Chapter Five, most teachers encourage students to visit them during their office hours or to make an appointment to see them when they have a question or problem. Whether they make an appointment or not, students are expected to make every effort to use this time as productively as possible.

First of all, before you knock on your teacher's door, plan what you are going to say. If necessary, write down your main points or questions and perhaps practice once before you go. During the meeting, be an active listener. Have a pen and paper ready to take notes. Ask questions when you don't understand; don't just nod and smile and leave without having understood. Finally, be aware of when it is time for you to leave. Leaving at the appropriate time will help you maintain a positive relationship with your teacher.

Activity 1: Brainstorming

In groups of four, brainstorm the following:

1. the reasons you might need to **apologize** to a teacher or a fellow student
2. the reasons you might need to **ask** for your teacher's **permission**
3. the different **signals** people use to show that they are **ready to end a conversation**
4. the signals a **teacher** might use to end a conversation

DIALOGUE ANALYSIS

Listen to the dialogue to understand why the students have come to Ms. Graves's office. Then listen again to complete the highlighting activity below.

Situation: Ms. Graves is holding office hours. Three students come to see her for various reasons.

(Knock, Knock)

Kenneth: Excuse me, Ms. Graves, but do you have a minute?

Ms. Graves: Sure, Kenneth, come in and have a seat. What can I do for you today?

Kenneth: Well, I'd like to talk to you about . . .

(Knock, Knock)

Ms. Graves: Yes, what is it?   5

Patti: Excuse me for interrupting, but could I talk to you for a minute?

Ms. Graves: Well, I'm rather busy at the moment. What would you like to talk about?

Patti: I'd like to ask your advice on something.

Ms. Graves: Okay, but could you wait outside for a few minutes? I'll be with   10 you as soon as I can.

Patti: All right. Thank you. (Leaves the office.)

Ms. Graves: Now what were you saying, Kenneth?

Kenneth: Well, I'd like to talk to you about . . .

(Knock, Knock)

Ms. Graves: Yes?   15

Anthony: I'm sorry to bother you, but do you have a minute? I have a small problem I'd like to discuss with you.

Ms. Graves: Well, I'm talking to Kenneth at the moment, and Patti is waiting outside to see me. Could you wait until she's finished?

Anthony: Well, actually I have biology class in a few minutes, so I'll come   20 back this afternoon. Is 2:00 okay?

Ms. Graves: Yes. I'll see you then. (Leaves.) I'm sorry, Kenneth, what were you saying?

Kenneth: Well, I wanted to talk to you about being late for class, but I've just remembered, Anthony and I are in the same biology class,   25 so could I come back this afternoon too?

Ms. Graves: Yes, why don't you come at 2:15 after I've finished with Anthony?

Kenneth: Okay. Thank you very much for your time. See you later.

Ms. Graves: Thanks for *your* time. Could you tell Patti to come in?   30

Activity 2: Highlighting

1. Highlight the expressions used by the students **to open a conversation.**
2. Highlight the expressions used by the students **to state their business.**
3. Highlight the expressions used **to close the conversation.**

 **Activity 3: Class Mingle**

- Your teacher will ask you to look at two pages in this book.
- Mix with the other students in the class and try to find the answers to the questions, advice, and problems on the pages that your teacher has asked you to look at.
- When a student answers your question, write the answer in the space provided.
- When someone asks you a question, look on your answer sheet for the answer.
- If you have the answer, give it to them.
- If you don't have the answer, say "I'm sorry. I don't know." or "I'm sorry, but I don't know anything about that."

- **Remember to use the appropriate expressions for opening a conversation, stating your business, and closing a conversation.**

PRACTICE 1: OPENING A CONVERSATION, STATING ONE'S BUSINESS, AND CLOSING A CONVERSATION

The purpose of Activity 3 is to practice using the expressions for opening a conversation, stating one's business, and closing a conversation.

Activity 3: STUDENT A

OPENING A CONVERSATION

"Excuse me, but do you have a minute?"

"I'm sorry to bother you, but do you have a minute?"

"Excuse me for interrupting, but could I talk to you for a minute?"

STATING ONE'S BUSINESS

QUESTION: "I'd like to talk to you about . . . "	ANSWERS
. . . geography. What is the capital of Mongolia?	_____
. . . evolution. When did Charles Darwin live?	_____
. . . authors. Who wrote the book *Great Expectations*?	_____
. . . chemistry. What is the symbol for the element copper?	_____

ADVICE: "I'd like to ask your advice on . . . "	ANSWERS
. . . hats. Mine doesn't fit properly. What should I do?	_____
. . . the costume party. I don't have a thing to wear! What should I do?	_____
. . . dancing. I keep stepping on toes. What should I do?	_____

PROBLEM: "I have a problem with my . . . "	ANSWERS
. . . reading homework. I forgot to write down the page numbers for tomorrow's homework.	_____
. . . science experiment. It didn't work.	_____
. . . finances. I've lost my wallet.	_____

CLOSING A CONVERSATION

"Well, thank you very much for your time."

"Well, I know you're busy. Thanks for your time."

If you don't have the answer, please say "I'm sorry. I don't know." or "I'm sorry, but I don't know anything about that."

ANSWERS TO QUESTIONS

TOPIC	ANSWER
Philosophy	from 1558 to 1679
Art	Pablo Picasso and Georges Braque
Roman mythology	Bacchus
Sports	Wimbledon

ADVICE

TOPIC	ADVICE
Head	Don't worry. That's normal.
Life	Why don't you join some clubs?
Car repair	Why don't you try jump starting it?

SOLUTIONS TO PROBLEMS

TOPIC	SOLUTION
Writing class	Why don't you share with a friend until it comes in?
Computer program	I'm afraid you'll have to find the mistake and fix it.
Dictionary	Why don't you check the lost and found?

Activity 3: STUDENT B

OPENING A CONVERSATION

"Excuse me, but do you have a minute?"

"I'm sorry to bother you, but do you have a minute?"

"Excuse me for interrupting, but could I talk to you for a minute?"

STATING ONE'S BUSINESS

QUESTION: "I'd like to talk to you about . . . "	ANSWERS
. . . philosophy. When did the English philosopher Hobbes live?	_____
. . . Italy. What color is the Italian flag?	_____
. . . fish. What is a "halibut"?	_____
. . . books. Who wrote *The Catcher in the Rye*?	_____

ADVICE: "I'd like to ask your advice on . . . "	ANSWERS
. . . keeping warm. My ears are too cold. What should I do?	_____
. . . life. My life is too boring. What should I do?	_____
. . . my essay. My essay is too short. What should I do?	_____

PROBLEM: "I have a problem with my . . . "	ANSWERS
. . . writing class. The bookstore has run out of the course textbook.	_____
. . . physics class. I'm not feeling well, so I'd like to go home early today.	_____
. . . history class. I can't understand what to do for homework.	_____

CLOSING A CONVERSATION

"Well, thank you very much for your time."

"Well, I know you're busy. Thanks for your time."

If you don't have the answer, please say "I'm sorry. I don't know." or "I'm sorry, but I don't know anything about that."

ANSWERS TO QUESTIONS

TOPIC	ANSWER
Ghana	Red, yellow, green, and black
Medicine	Chloroquine
Authors	Charles Dickens
Geography	Ulan Bator

ADVICE

TOPIC	ADVICE
the costume party	Why don't you borrow a costume from me?
Dancing	Why don't you take dance classes?
Feet	Why don't you sit down?
Haircuts	Why don't you go to the *Hair Pare*?

SOLUTIONS TO PROBLEMS

TOPIC	SOLUTION
Finances	Why don't you go to the lost and found?
Psychology class	Yes. Why don't you come back this afternoon?
Sociology class	Don't forget to do tomorrow's homework.

Activity 3: STUDENT C

OPENING A CONVERSATION

"Excuse me, but do you have a minute?"
"I'm sorry to bother you, but do you have a minute?"
"Excuse me for interrupting, but could I talk to you for a minute?"

STATING ONE'S BUSINESS

QUESTION: "I'd like to talk to you about . . . "	ANSWERS
. . . Ghana. What color is the flag of Ghana?	_____
. . . religion. In what year were the Dead Sea Scrolls found?	_____
. . . art. Which two artists started the Cubist movement?	_____
. . . sports. What is the oldest tennis tournament in the world?	_____

ADVICE: "I'd like to ask your advice on . . . "	ANSWERS
. . . money. I found $500 on the road. What should I do?	_____
. . . car repair. My car won't start. What should I do?	_____
. . . haircuts. I'd like to get a haircut. Where should I go?	_____

PROBLEM: "I have a problem with my . . . "	ANSWERS
. . . psychology class. I missed the quiz yesterday. Can I make it up?	_____
. . . computer program. I spent four hours writing my program, but it doesn't work.	_____
. . . library search. I've been looking for a book, but I can't find it.	_____

CLOSING A CONVERSATION

"Well, thank you very much for your time."
"Well, I know you're busy. Thanks for your time."

If you don't have the answer, please say "I'm sorry. I don't know." or "I'm sorry, but I don't know anything about that."

ANSWERS TO QUESTIONS

TOPIC	*ANSWER*
Fish	A flat fish found in deep, cold seas
Argentina	Buenos Aires
Astronomy	Ursa Major
Evolution	1809 to 1882

ADVICE

TOPIC	*ADVICE*
Wine	Why don't you ask your liquor store clerk?
Shoes	Why don't you get your eyes tested?
Essay	Why don't you add more detail?

SOLUTIONS TO PROBLEMS

TOPIC	*SOLUTION*
Science experiment	That's okay, but I'm afraid you'll have to do it again.
Physics class	Okay, but remember to get today's notes from a friend.
Essay assignment	Try to finish it as soon as possible.

Activity 3: STUDENT D

OPENING A CONVERSATION

"Excuse me, but do you have a minute?"

"I'm sorry to bother you, but do you have a minute?"

"Excuse me for interrupting, but could I talk to you for a minute?"

STATING ONE'S BUSINESS

QUESTION: "I'd like to talk to you about . . . "	ANSWERS
. . . astronomy. What is another name for "the big dipper"?	_____
. . . medicine. What drug is often used to prevent malaria?	_____
. . . Argentina. What is the capital of Argentina?	_____
. . . Roman mythology. Who was the Roman god of wine?	_____

ADVICE: "I'd like to ask your advice on . . . "	ANSWERS
. . . wine. I'm having a dinner party and don't know about wines. What should I do?	_____
. . . feet. My feet hurt. What should I do?	_____
. . . shoes. My shoes don't match. What should I do?	_____

PROBLEM: "I have a problem with my . . . "	ANSWERS
. . . dictionary. I've lost it.	_____
. . . essay assignment. It is due today, but I haven't finished it.	_____
. . . sociology class. I missed class this morning.	_____

CLOSING A CONVERSATION

"Well, thank you very much for your time."

"Well, I know you're busy. Thanks for your time."

If you don't have the answer, please say "I'm sorry. I don't know." or "I'm sorry, but I don't know anything about that."

ANSWERS TO QUESTIONS

TOPIC	ANSWER
Italy	Green, white, and red
Books	J. D. Salinger
Religion	in 1947
Chemistry	Cu

ADVICE

TOPIC	ADVICE
Hats	Why don't you buy a new one?
Money	Why don't you take it to the police station?
Keeping warm	Why don't you put on your hat?

SOLUTIONS TO PROBLEMS

TOPIC	SOLUTION
Reading homework	The assignment was to read pages 10 to 14.
History class	You need to prepare a presentation for next week.
Library search	Why don't you ask the librarian to help you?

Activity 4: Listening

Listen to the dialogue and put a ✓ next to the expressions that you hear. Then check your answers against the dialogue on the next page. Finally, practice the dialogue with your partner.

Apologizing

_____ I'm sorry . . .
_____ I'm very sorry . . .
_____ I'm really sorry . . .
_____ I'm awfully sorry . . .
_____ I'm terribly sorry . . .

Giving Reasons

+ { _____ . . . but . . .
_____ . . . but I have to . . .
_____ . . . but I had to . . . }

Asking permission

_____ Can I . . . ?
_____ Could I . . . ?
_____ Do you mind if I . . . ?
_____ Is it all right to . . . ?
_____ Would it be possible
      for me to . . . ?

+ { _____ . . . because . . .
_____ . . . because I have to . . . }

DIALOGUE

Situation: Gerhard has come to talk to his teacher, Dr. Chenoweth.

Gerhard: I'm sorry to bother you, Dr. Chenoweth, but do you have a minute?

Dr. Chenoweth: Sure Gerhard, what can I do for you today?

Gerhard: Well, I'm sorry that I missed class this morning, but I had to walk the dog because my younger brother who usually does 5 it was sick and my mother who would have walked him was taking care of my brother, so I had to do it.

Dr. Chenoweth: I see . . . but didn't you miss class last week because your dog died?

Gerhard: Uhhh. That was the other one. 10

Dr. Chenoweth: I see.

Gerhard: Also, I'm very sorry, but I have to take care of the dog and my brother tonight, so I won't be able to finish my essay on time.

Dr. Chenoweth: I see. 15

Gerhard: And another thing . . . I'm awfully sorry about this, but do you mind if I miss tomorrow's quiz because I have to go to my second cousin's wife's wedding.

Dr. Chenoweth: Your second cousin's wife's wedding? Wife . . . doesn't that mean she's already married? 20

Gerhard: Yes, but she got divorced.

Dr. Chenoweth: Well, actually I do mind. It's an important quiz.

Gerhard: Well, would it be possible for me to take it another time?

Dr. Chenoweth: Yes, it would. When are you free?

Gerhard: Free . . . mmm . . . soccer match tomorrow . . . party on 25 Friday . . . walk the dog . . . haircut . . . date with Sally . . . wash the car . . . Er . . . Could I do it two weeks from Friday, just after the end of the term?

Dr. Chenoweth: Well. Gerhard, don't you think that would be a bit late?

Gerhard: I'm really sorry, but that seems to be the only time I'm 30 free . . .

Activity 5: Class Mingle

Now that we have identified the expressions that are commonly used for apologizing, asking permission, and giving reasons, we will practice using them.

- Your teacher will give you a strip of paper. On the paper will be written a partial sentence.
- Mix with the other students in the class.
- When you meet another student, make a sentence, using the partial sentence on the strip of paper and the language you heard in Activity 4 for apologizing, asking permission, and giving reasons.
- Listen to your partner's sentence and respond in some way. For example, you could choose one of the following:

Asking Permission	Apologizing
Yes, you may. Yes, that's fine (with me). No, I'm sorry. I can't allow you to do that.	That's okay. Try to . . . I see. Maybe you could . . . I'm sorry, but that's not acceptable. I'm afraid I'm going to have to . . .

- After both of you have made sentences, exchange strips.
- Continue to meet, make sentences, and exchange strips until your teacher tells you to stop.

Activity 6: Listening

1. Listen to the dialogue once and answer the following question:
   What does Dr. Chenoweth want Gerhard to do?
2. Listen to the dialogue again and fill in the missing expressions below.
3. Listen again and check your answers.

Situation: . . . 15 minutes later Gerhard is still in Dr. Chenoweth's office.

Gerhard: . . . so I'm really sorry about all the trouble I've caused.

Dr. Chenoweth: Yes . . . Well . . . (1) _____. As I said before, if you can finish all 12 essays before tomorrow at 4 o'clock, you may be able to pass the course.

Gerhard: Well, I'm sure I can. I just have a small party this evening, and I'm going to a soccer match with a friend in the morning, but . . .

Dr. Chenoweth: Yes . . . well . . . then (2) _____ ?

Gerhard: Yes, but I might not be able to come at exactly 4 o'clock.

Dr. Chenoweth: Don't worry about it. Just come when you can. (3) _____ ?

Gerhard: Well, they're not exactly questions . . .

Dr. Chenoweth: Good, (4) _____

Gerhard: Uhhh. All 12?

Dr. Chenoweth: Yes. Gerhard. (5) _____ ?

Gerhard: By 4 o'clock?

Dr. Chenoweth: That's right. (6) _____ , Gerhard.

PRACTICE 3: KNOWING WHEN IT'S TIME TO LEAVE

The purpose of Activity 6 is to learn to recognize the language used to tell someone that it is time for a meeting to end. In particular, you will learn how to know when it is time to leave a teacher's office.

Gerhard: Umm. About the final exam . . .

Dr. Chenoweth: Good-bye Gerhard.

Gerhard: But will it be . . .   20

Dr. Chenoweth: Gerhard, get out!!!

Notice that the teacher uses three strategies:

- **Thanking the student.**
- **Asking for any final questions.**
- **Using the past tense.**

CHAPTER ASSIGNMENT: VISITING A TEACHER'S OFFICE

 Activity 7: Role Play

STUDENT A

Working with a partner, role play the following situations.

Role Play 1

You are a student. You have just finished writing an outline for your next essay, but you aren't sure about whether it is well-organized or not. You would like your teacher to look at it before you start writing your essay.

Role Play 2

You are a teacher. One of your students has come to talk with you. Give advice.

Role Play 3

You are a student. You are having difficulty making friends on campus. Ask your teacher for some advice.

Role Play 4

You are a teacher. One of your students has come to talk with you. Suggest some extra reading, if you can.

Role Play 5

You are a student. You need to leave the country for a few weeks in order to take care of some family business. Explain to your teacher that you have to go and ask what you can do to make up the work that you will miss.

Role Play 6

You are a teacher. One of your students has come to talk with you. If the student is believable, give an extension.

Role Play 7

You are a student. You weren't able to hand in your homework yesterday, so you have come to your teacher's office to hand it in today. Apologize and explain that you were sick.

Role Play 8

You are a teacher. One of your students has come to talk with you. If you think the student has a good reason, arrange for a make-up time.

CHAPTER ASSIGNMENT: VISITING A TEACHER'S OFFICE

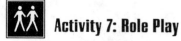 **Activity 7: Role Play**

STUDENT B

Working with a partner, role play the following situations.

Role Play 1

You are a teacher. One of your students has come to talk with you. Look at the student's outline and give some advice.

Role Play 2

You are a student. You are worried because your reading ability does not seem to be improving. Ask your teacher for advice.

Role Play 3

You are a teacher. One of your students has come to talk with you. Try to give some useful suggestions.

Role Play 4

You are a student. Your teacher mentioned a topic in class that you are very interested in. Ask your teacher for some extra reading on the topic.

Role Play 5

You are a teacher. One of your students has come to talk with you. Give some instructions for making up the missed work.

Role Play 6

A member of your family has been very sick lately and you have been responsible for taking care of her. As a result, you haven't been able to complete your research paper on time. Explain this to your teacher, and ask if you can have an extension.

Role Play 7

You are a teacher. One of your students has come to talk with you. If the student is believable, accept the homework and give the student the next assignment.

Role Play 8

You were late to class today, so you missed a quiz. You have come to your teacher's office to apologize, explain why you were late, and to see if your teacher will allow you to make up the quiz.

CHAPTER SIX: *Summary of Key Language*

OPENING A CONVERSATION

Excuse me, but do you have a minute?

I'm sorry to bother you, but do you have a minute?

Excuse me for interrupting, but could I talk to you for a minute?

STATING ONE'S BUSINESS

I'd like to talk to you about . . .

I have a small problem I'd like to discuss with you.

I'd like to ask your advice on something.

CLOSING A CONVERSATION

Well, thank you very much for your time.

Well, I know you're busy. Thanks for your time.

APOLOGIZING

I'm (very/really/awfully) sorry.

ASKING PERMISSION

Can I . . . ?

Could I . . . ?

Do you mind if I . . . ?

Is it all right to . . . ?

Would it be possible for me to . . . ?

GIVING REASONS

. . . but . . . (I have/had to) . . .

. . . because . . . (I have/had to) . . .

OTHER

UNIT ASSIGNMENT: VISITING A TEACHER'S OFFICE

As the unit assignment for Unit 3, you will be asked to visit a teacher's office. Before you go, read and make sure that you understand the following evaluation form, which summarizes the main points of this unit. Also, make sure that you are fully prepared and that you take your book with you to your teacher's office so that your teacher can use this form to evaluate your performance.

✓ – = *needs improvement*
✓ = *okay*
✓ + = *very good*

EVALUATION FORM

_____ Found out if the teacher was busy.

_____ Waited to be offered a seat.

_____ Arranged an appointment for a later time if necessary.

_____ Stated the purpose of the visit.

_____ Was prepared to take notes if necessary.

_____ Participated actively.

     _____ a) Asked for clarification when necessary.
     _____ b) Used active listening skills.
     _____ c) Used eye contact effectively.

_____ Understood when it was time to leave.

_____ Thanked the teacher.

COMMENTS:

UNIT 4
The Group Discussion

UNIT OUTLINE

Chapter Seven: **PARTICIPATING IN A GROUP DISCUSSION**

    Introduction
    Dialogue Analysis
    Practice 1: Giving an Opinion, Agreeing
    Practice 2: Disagreeing Politely
    Chapter Assignment: Resolving Differences
    Summary of Key Language

Chapter Eight: **LEADING A GROUP DISCUSSION**

    Introduction
    Dialogue Analysis
    Practice 1: Introducing a Topic, Moving on to a New Topic
    Practice 2: Asking for an Opinion, Responding, Summarizing,
        Moving on to a New Topic
    Chapter Assignment: Mock Discussion
    Summary of Key Language

Chapter Nine: REPORTING ON A GROUP DISCUSSION

Introduction
Practice 1: Organizing a Summary
Practice 2: Preparing a Summary
Chapter Assignment: Reporting on a Group Discussion
Summary of Key Language

UNIT ASSIGNMENT: The Group Discussion

Chapter Seven

Participating in a Group Discussion

INTRODUCTION

In classes and in social encounters, students are expected to give opinions on a wide range of topics and to agree and disagree with the opinions offered by others. By giving opinions in an accepted way, we invite others to agree or disagree with us, making a conversation interesting and informative.

Giving opinions and agreeing are relatively easy tasks. However, when disagreeing the potential to insult or offend the speaker is much greater, so it is important to disagree in a polite and respectful way. This chapter of Unit 4 focuses on how to give an opinion, agree and disagree politely. Mastering these skills will help you participate actively and confidently in discussions in class and elsewhere on campus.

Activity 1: Brainstorming

In the space provided below, list as many expressions as you can for *giving an opinion*, *agreeing*, and *disagreeing*.

Giving an Opinion	Agreeing	Disagreeing

DIALOGUE ANALYSIS

Listen to the dialogue one time for a general understanding. Then listen again to complete Activity 2.

Situation: Students in a current affairs class are discussing problems facing the U.S.A. today. When all the groups have finished, they will present a summary of their discussion to the rest of the class. Nanci is the group leader.

Nanci: Okay, so today we need to discuss problems in the United States. Ken, what do you think is the worst problem facing America today?

Ken: Well, in my opinion, it's violence. Too many people are hurt or often killed each year in violent crimes.

Tony: Yes, that's true, but what about racism? As far as I'm concerned, racism is one of the major causes of violence today. ₅

Nanci: Yes, you both have a point, but it seems to me that there are some problems that have a greater impact on everybody. For example, if we destroy the earth, we won't be able to survive as a species.

Ken: Yes, you may be right, but how can we survive in a violent world? ₁₀ In my opinion, it's not worth saving the world if we can't eradicate the violence.

Tony: That may be, but even if we eliminated violence, we'd still have the problem of racism.

Nanci: Yes, that's true, but you have to remember that saving the environ- ₁₅ ment may be our only choice. Problems such as violence and racism will take a long time to solve, and we won't get the chance to solve them unless we start thinking more about the environment.

Ken: Yes, I see what you mean. Perhaps you're right. Protecting the earth buys us some time. ₂₀

Tony: Yes, I see your point. It seems to me, however, that while you may be right that the environment presents the most immediate problem, I still feel that the problem of racism is fundamentally more important for mankind.

Nanci: Okay, do we all agree that the environment prob- ₂₅ lem is the most *immediate* problem facing the U.S.?

Ken: Yes, I agree.

Tony: Yes, I think so too.

Nanci: All right. Then what about Tony's point about ₃₀ racism being more fundamentally important? Ken . . .

Activity 2: Highlighting

1. Using a highlighter, mark the expressions that the speakers use to *give an opinion*.
2. Mark the expressions that the speakers use to *agree*.
3. Mark the expressions that the speakers use to *disagree*.

 Activity 3: Class Mingle

- Your teacher will give you a strip of paper with an opinion written on it.
- Stand up and mingle with the other students in the class.
- Use one of the expressions below to give your opinion to whomever you meet.
- Try to use each expression several times.

- When other students give an opinion, please agree with them using the expressions listed below.
- Again, try to use as many expressions as you can.

Remember:

- Your tone of voice will indicate strong or weak agreement.
- If you don't agree completely, you can add *"well"* or *"mmm"* at the beginning of your statement to weaken your agreement.

Key Language

Giving an Opinion	Agreeing
I think . . .	Yes, I see what you mean.
I feel . . .	Yes, that's true.
It seems to me that . . .	I agree.
As far as I'm concerned . . .	You're right.
In my opinion . . .	Yes, I think so too.
	I completely agree.
	Exactly!

PRACTICE 1: GIVING AN OPINION, AGREEING

The purpose of Activity 3 is to practice giving opinions and agreeing with other people's opinions.

PRACTICE 2: DISAGREEING POLITELY

The purpose of Activity 4 is to practice disagreeing with other people in a polite way.

 Activity 4: Pairwork Discussions

- On the next page are two issues for you to discuss with your partner, using the list of pros and cons provided.
- Your partner will have the opposite point of view.
- You may also add some reasons of your own.
- After you have finished the first discussion move on to the second one.
- In your discussion, remember to use the appropriate expressions for *giving an opinion* and *disagreeing*.

Giving an Opinion	*Disagreeing*
I think . . .	Yes, but . . .
I feel . . .	I agree, but . . .
It seems to me that . . .	That may be, but . . .
As far as I'm concerned . . .	You may be right, but . . .
In my opinion . . .	I see your point, but . . .
	Yes, but don't you think that . . . ?
	Yes, but you have to remember . . .
	I don't quite agree. What about . . .?
	I'm not so sure I agree. I . . .
	You have a point, but . . .

NOTE: The word *but* may be replaced by the word *however* in any of the expressions above.

Activity 4: STUDENT A

1. Mothers should work outside the home.

PROS

- *can earn more money*
- *children can learn to be independent*
- *husbands have the opportunity to cook*
- *husbands have the opportunity to clean the house*
- *more equality between men and women*
- *a woman can lead a more interesting life*
- *Other?*

---

2. Public transportation in major cities should run all night.

CONS

- *people who live near noisy train tracks can't sleep*
- *it encourages people to stay out too late, so they may be too tired to get to work on time the next day*
- *train and bus maintenance becomes difficult*
- *late- night safety becomes a problem*
- *transportation employees have to work at night*
- *taxi companies will go out of business*
- *Other?*

Activity 4: STUDENT B

1. Mothers should work outside the home.

CONS

- *mothers will be overworked*
- *family relationships are more important than money*
- *children will not eat properly*
- *the husband may be tired from doing his job and doing the cooking*
- *the relationship between mother and child becomes weaker*
- *the house will be untidy*
- *children's education will suffer*
- *Other?*

---

2. Public transportation in major cities should run all night.

PROS

- *people can stay out as late as they want*
- *staying out late helps the economy*
- *taking public transportation saves natural resources*
- *people who have to work late at night can still go out after work*
- *Other?*

CHAPTER ASSIGNMENT: RESOLVING DIFFERENCES

 Activity 5: Role Play

STUDENT A

In your *preparation group* of three to five students, read the following three situations. In the first situation, you are the husband. In the second, you are the mother, and in third you are the daughter. With the other members of your group, brainstorm possible reasons for each of these character's opinions, and write them below each situation in the space provided. Then, your teacher will ask you to *form a pair with a student from another group* and role play the three situations. You may be asked to perform your role play for the class, so be creative and have fun!

ROLE ONE: THE HUSBAND

A husband and wife are talking together. The husband has just been offered a job overseas. He has always wanted to live abroad, and he believes that this move would be an excellent career opportunity. His wife, however, doesn't want to go. Play the role of the husband.

Notes:

ROLE TWO: THE MOTHER

A mother and her 20-year-old daughter are talking together. The daughter is explaining to her mother that she wants to move out of the house and live on her own. Her mother thinks that this is a bad idea. Play the role of the mother.

Notes:

ROLE THREE: THE DAUGHTER

A father and his 18-year-old daughter are talking together. The daughter wants to go to college in a foreign country. However, her father thinks that it would be better for her to study in her own country. Play the role of the daughter.

Notes:

CHAPTER ASSIGNMENT: RESOLVING DIFFERENCES

Activity 5: Role Play

STUDENT B

In your *preparation group* of three to five students, read the following three situations. In the first situation, you are the wife. In the second, you are the daughter, and in third you are the father. With the other members of your group, brainstorm possible reasons for each of these character's opinions, and write them below each situation in the space provided. Then, your teacher will ask you to *form a pair with a student from another group* and role play the three situations. You may be asked to perform your role play for the class, so be creative and have fun!

ROLE ONE: THE WIFE

A husband and wife are talking together. The husband has just been offered a job overseas. He has always wanted to live abroad, and he believes that this move would be an excellent career opportunity. His wife, however, doesn't want to go. Play the role of the wife.

Notes:

ROLE TWO: THE DAUGHTER

A mother and her 20-year-old daughter are talking together. The daughter is explaining to her mother that she wants to move out of the house and live on her own. Her mother thinks that this is a bad idea. Play the role of the daughter.

Notes:

ROLE THREE: THE FATHER

A father and his 18-year-old daughter are talking together. The daughter wants to go to college in a foreign country. However, her father thinks that it would be better for her to study in her own country. Play the role of the father.

Notes:

CHAPTER SEVEN: *Summary of Key Language*

GIVING AN OPINION

I think . . .

I feel . . .

It seems to me that . . .

As far as I'm concerned . . .

In my opinion . . .

AGREEING

Yes, I see what you mean.

That's true.

I agree.

Yes, maybe you're right.

Yes, I think so too.

I completely agree.

Exactly!

OTHER

DISAGREEING

Yes, but . . .

I agree, but . . .

That may be, but . . .

You may be right, but . . .

I see your point, but . . .

Yes, but don't you think that . . . ?

Yes, but you have to remember that . . .

I don't quite agree. What about . . . ?

I'm not so sure I agree. I . . .

You (both) have a point, but . . .

Chapter Eight

Leading a Group Discussion

INTRODUCTION

The group discussion is perhaps the most common academic speaking activity that students undertake in class. Being an active participant in a group discussion, which was dealt with in Chapter Seven of this unit, is essential for a successful discussion to take place. However, having all members of a group participate actively is not enough to ensure a successful discussion. Any group, especially an active one, requires a leader to make sure that the discussion has an aim, remains focused, keeps going, and comes to an acceptable conclusion. The group leader is also responsible for choosing a secretary to take notes on what has been said and for making sure that all group members have a chance to express their opinions.

Activity 1: Pairwork Discussion

1. Look at the introduction above and highlight the responsibilities of a group leader.
2. Discuss each of the responsibilities with your partner and make sure that you understand the meaning of each one.
3. Discuss how you might carry out each of these responsibilities if you were a group leader.

DIALOGUE ANALYSIS

 Activity 2: Listening

You will hear two dialogues. While you are listening, think about the differences between Dialogue 1 and Dialogue 2. Pay special attention to the group leader.

Situation: Four students are having a group discussion. The group leader is Georgina; the other participants are Johnathan, Paula, and Richard. The topic is the Beatles.

DIALOGUE 1

Georgina:	Okay, the best Beatles song. How about *Yesterday?*	
Paula:	Yes, it's good.	
Richard:	Yes.	
Johnathan:	Yes, but so is *Yellow Submarine.*	
Paula:	Mmm.	5
Georgina:	So, *Yellow Submarine* and *Yesterday.*	
Richard:	*Hey Jude.*	
Georgina:	Yes. Erm . . . , mmm . . .	
Paula:	[Silence]	
Georgina:	Johnathan?	10
Johnathan:	[Silence]	
Georgina:	Anybody else?	
Others:	[Silence]	
Georgina:	What about *She Loves You?*	
Johnathan:	Yeah.	15
Paula:	Yeah.	
Richard:	Yeah.	
Georgina:	HELP!	

DIALOGUE 2

Georgina: Today, we need to decide what the best Beatles song is. Let's begin with *Yesterday.* What do you think, Paula?

Paula: I think it's certainly one of the best. The music is beautiful, and the words are so deep.

Richard: I see your point, but isn't it a song of the past?   5

Johnathan: Yes, and I don't think it's as good as *Yellow Submarine. Yellow Submarine* is one of the best songs ever.

Paula: I agree it's a good song, but it's not very colorful, is it?

Georgina: Okay, so far we have *Yesterday* and *Yellow Submarine.* Does anybody have anything else to add?   10

Richard: As far as I'm concerned, they're both too sentimental. I prefer *Hey Jude.* The drumming's brilliant!

Georgina: Yes, that's a good point. Would anybody like to comment on what Richard's just said?

Paula: Yes, *Hey Jude* is an excellent song, but it's not as good as   15 *Yesterday.*

Georgina: What do you think, Johnathan?

Johnathan: I agree; it is a good song, but *Yellow Submarine* is far better.

Georgina: Well, there seems to be some disagreement there. Richard, do you have anything else to add?   20

Richard: No.

Georgina: What about *She Loves You?*

Johnathan: Yeah, yeah, yeah.
Paula: Yeah, yeah, yeah. } (All together)
Richard: Yeah, yeah, yeah.   25

Georgina: Okay, so we all agree that *She Loves You* is the best Beatles song. Let's move on to the next point. We need to discuss Beatles movies. Richard, what's your opinion of *Help?*

Activity 3: Highlighting

Reread Dialogue 2 on page 111, highlight the expressions used by the group leader to guide the discussion, and number them according to the five categories listed below.

1. Introducing a topic
2. Asking for an opinion
3. Responding
4. Summarizing
5. Moving on to a new topic

Next, working in groups of three or four, brainstorm other expressions that can be used for each of these.

PRACTICE 1: INTRODUCING A TOPIC, MOVING ON TO A NEW TOPIC

The purpose of Activity 4 is to practice the language needed for introducing a new topic and for moving on to a new topic.

Activity 4: Groupwork—Categorizing

- In this activity you will be working in groups of four or five.
- Your teacher will give each student in your group a different list of topics.
- Your task is to give the other students in your group hints so that they can guess the topics you have on your list.
- The hints must be within the category of your topic. For example, if one of the topics on your list is *Months*, then you can give hints, such as *June, September, May*. However, most of the topics won't be as easy as this.
- Take turns giving hints and guessing the answers.

To introduce your topic and to move on to the next topic you should use the appropriate language for *introducing a topic* and *moving on to a new topic* that you highlighted and discussed in the last activity. Use the dialogue below to help you.

A: **Today we need to discuss** _____*_____ .
         Let's begin with ____*June*____ .

B: Girls' names.

A: **How about** _*September*_ ?

C: Months of the year.

A: **Okay, we agree that** the answer is *months of the year* .
         Let's move on to the next topic.

* = Don't mention the real topic, just cough, or say "something."

Activity 5: Groupwork—Opinions

- In this activity you will work in groups of four or five, taking turns being the group leader.
- First, look at the dialogue outline below.
- The outline contains the language that the group leader will need to **ask for opinions** from other members of the group, to **summarize the opinions** of the group, and to **move on to the next topic.**
- Each member of the group will be given a role card that contains a statement and a number of questions.
- After looking at the dialogue for a few minutes, Student A should begin as the group leader by reading the statement on the role card and asking for opinions from the other members of the group.
- As the group leader, remember to **keep the conversation going** and **make sure that everyone has a chance to speak.** To do this, you may need to use the questions provided on the role card.
- At the end of the discussion, remember to **summarize the main points** and **move on to the next topic.**
- For the next topic, Student B should act as the group leader.

PRACTICE 2: ASKING FOR AN OPINION, RESPONDING, SUMMARIZING, MOVING ON TO A NEW TOPIC

The purpose of Activity 5 is to practice the language needed for asking for an opinion, responding, summarizing, and moving on to a new topic.

Group Leader:	(STATEMENT)
Respondent 1:	(OPINION/RESPONSE)
Group Leader:	**What do you think about that?**
Respondent 2:	(OPINION/RESPONSE)
Group Leader:	**What do you think, [name]?**
Respondent 3:	(OPINION/RESPONSE)
Group Leader:	**Would you like to comment on what [name] has just said?**
Respondent:	(OPINION/RESPONSE)
Group Leader:	**Does anyone have anything else to add?**
Respondent:	(OPINION/RESPONSE, IF ANY)
Group Leader:	**Okay, so far we've said _____ . Let's move on to the next topic.**

CHAPTER ASSIGNMENT: MOCK DISCUSSION

 Activity 6: Role Play

STUDENT A

Working in groups of three, you will have three mock discussions. In one of the discussions you will be the group leader, while in the other two you will be a participant. Remember to use the language that you have learned for leading a group discussion and for participating in a group discussion.

ROLE ONE: GROUP LEADER

You are the group leader. The topic for discussion is whether or not women should work outside the home. Your responsibility is to keep the conversation going and to make sure that the other group members speak for equal amounts of time. Try to bring the discussion to a conclusion.

Be sure to use the key language that we have learned for being an effective group leader.

ROLE TWO: PARTICIPANT

You believe that all high school students **should** be required to wear uniforms because:

- it increases morale
- it provides a sense of school identity
- it helps students focus on their schoolwork rather than on their appearances
- it is less distracting for teachers
- it keeps costs down
- other?

Be sure to use the key language that we have learned for giving an opinion, agreeing, and disagreeing.

ROLE THREE: PARTICIPANT

You believe that cigarette smoking should **not** be banned in public places. It should be a matter of choice because:

- cigarette smoking allows for human individuality
- other things that are more harmful are not banned
- cigarette smoking reduces stress
- cigarette sales increase tax revenue
- other

Be sure to use the key language that we have learned for giving an opinion, agreeing, and disagreeing.

CHAPTER ASSIGNMENT: MOCK DISCUSSION

 Activity 6: Role Play

STUDENT B

Working in groups of three, you will have three mock discussions. In one of the discussions you will be the group leader, while in the other two you will be a participant. Remember to use the language that you have learned for leading a group discussion and for participating in a group discussion.

ROLE ONE: PARTICIPANT

You believe that women should **not** work outside the home because:
- they should take care of children
- it's natural for women to stay home
- women are better at housework
- it's embarrassing for a man if his wife works
- a clear division of labor leads to a more stable society
- other?

Be sure to use the key language that we have learned for giving an opinion, agreeing, and disagreeing.

ROLE TWO: GROUP LEADER

You are the group leader. **The topic for discussion is whether or not uniforms should be required for high school students.** Your responsibility is to keep the conversation going and to make sure that the other group members speak for equal amounts of time. Try to bring the discussion to a conclusion.

Be sure to use the key language that we have learned for being an effective group leader.

ROLE THREE: PARTICIPANT

You believe that cigarette smoking **should** be banned in public places because:
- smoking is dangerous to others
- smoking threatens our right to breathe clean air
- smoking causes cancer and therefore increases health costs
- discarded cigarettes are dirty and may cause fires
- other?

Be sure to use the key language that we have learned for giving an opinion, agreeing, and disagreeing.

CHAPTER ASSIGNMENT: MOCK DISCUSSION

 Activity 6: Role Play

STUDENT C

Working in groups of three, you will have three mock discussions. In one of the discussions you will be the group leader, while in the other two you will be a participant. Remember to use the language that you have learned for leading a group discussion and for participating in a group discussion.

ROLE ONE: PARTICIPANT

You believe that women **should** work outside the home because:
- women can contribute to society in positive ways
- it makes women feel good
- it brings in more income
- children can learn to be responsible
- it allows men to experience doing housework and spend time with children
- other?

Be sure to use the key language that we have learned for giving an opinion, agreeing, and disagreeing.

ROLE TWO: PARTICIPANT

You believe that high school students should **not** be required to wear uniforms because:
- high school students are mature enough to make their own decisions
- uniforms are boring
- a choice of clothing allows for individual freedom
- students can choose their clothing to suit the season
- teachers can recognize students more easily if they don't all dress the same
- other?

Be sure to use the key language that we have learned for giving an opinion, agreeing, and disagreeing.

ROLE THREE: GROUP LEADER

You are the group leader. The topic for discussion is whether or not cigarettes should be banned in public **places.** Your responsibility is to keep the conversation going and to make sure that the other group members speak for equal amounts of time. Try to bring the discussion to a conclusion.

Be sure to use the key language that we have learned for being an effective group leader.

CHAPTER EIGHT: *Summary of Key Language*

INTRODUCING A TOPIC

Today/First/Second we need to discuss/decide/prepare . . .

Let's begin with . . .

ASKING FOR AN OPINION

What about . . .?

How about . . . ?

What do you think, [name]?

What do you think about that?

Would anybody like to add to what [name] has just said?

Would anybody like to comment on what [name] has just said?

Does anybody have anything else to add?

[Name], what's your opinion of . . . ?

RESPONDING

That's an interesting point/idea/opinion.

Yes, that's a good point.

I never thought of that.

SUMMARIZING

Okay, so far we've said . . .

Okay, so far we have . . .

To sum up, we've said . . .

Well, there seems to be some
    disagreement there.

MOVING ON TO A NEW TOPIC

Okay, so we're all agreed that . . .

Okay, so we all agree that . . .

Okay, do we all agree that . . . ?

Okay, let's move on to the next point.

OTHER

Chapter Nine

Reporting on a Group Discussion

WELL, WE DISCUSSED THE TOPIC OF 'BREEDISM.' IN OUR DISCUSSION WE WERE TRYING TO DECIDE WHETHER OR NOT WE HELD STEREOTYPICAL VIEWS ABOUT OTHER DOGS. FIFI THOUGHT THAT SOME DOGS, SUCH AS MONGRELS, WERE UNSUITABLE FOR THE UNIVERSITY. ROVER THOUGHT POODLES WERE GENERALLY VAIN, AND LASSY ADDED THAT ST BERNARDS TENDED TO DRINK TOO MUCH. FANG MAINTAINED THAT NOT ALL ROTTWEILERS WERE VIOLENT, AND NOBODY DISAGREED WITH HIM!

INTRODUCTION

Participating in and leading a group discussion, presented in Chapters Seven and Eight of this unit, are two skills that are necessary for a successful group discussion. In addition to the roles of participant and group leader, one more member, the group secretary, plays an important role. The secretary is responsible for taking notes during the discussion and for reporting the main ideas to the rest of the class.

The role of the secretary involves three main tasks: taking notes, preparing a brief oral report, and presenting the report to the class. This chapter will introduce these skills and provide an opportunity for you to practice them.

PRACTICE 1: ORGANIZING A SUMMARY

The purpose of the following three activities is to give you practice in preparing summaries of group discussions, in order to be able to report on what was said.

 Activity 1: Listening

Listen to the second Beatles dialogue from Chapter Eight (page 111) again. As you listen, take notes on the main points in preparation for writing a summary.

Name of Participant	Opinion

 Activity 2: Summarizing

1. On a separate piece of paper, write a summary of the main points of the discussion. The group secretary for this particular discussion was Richard, so you should write the summary from his perspective. If you feel that a particular opinion was strongly put or that it is important to mention a particular person, then use that person's name when reporting. If this is not the case, then use the passive voice or pronouns, such as *somebody, nobody,* and *everybody.* Use the following tips and key language to help you.

Tips for Writing a Summary

When writing a summary, remember to:

- be brief
- include only those ideas that were discussed by the group
- include the most important information only
- exclude information that might embarrass a group member

Key Language

Introducing a Topic	Reporting Opinions	Concluding a Report
On the topic of _____ we . . . On the subject of ___ we . . . In our discussion we talked about . . . We were trying to decide . . . We discussed . . .	[name] thought that . . . [name] argued that . . . [name] added that . . . [name] suggested that . . . [name] put forward the idea that . . . This was supported by [name]	We came to the conclusion that . . . We decided that . . . Thank you.

2. Now, compare your summary with the one below. In particular, pay attention to the key language used to report the main points.

Summary of Beatles Dialogue

In our discussion we were trying to decide what was the best Beatles song ever. We discussed a number of possibilities including *Hey Jude, Yesterday* and *Yellow Submarine*. Paula pointed out that *Yesterday* was the best because of the combination of the melody and the lyrics. However, Johnathan argued that it was a song of the past and suggested that *Yellow Submarine* was better. *Hey Jude* was suggested as a possibility due to the excellent drumming involved. There was general agreement on this point, but *Yesterday* and *Yellow Submarine* were still felt to be better by some members of the group. At this point *She Loves You* was put forward by Georgina as a possible candidate. This suggestion was supported by the whole group. As a result we decided that *She Loves You* was our choice as the best Beatles song ever.

 Activity 3: Highlighting

Highlight the key language used to:

- introduce the topic
- report the opinions of the group members
- conclude the report

PRACTICE 2: PREPARING A SUMMARY

The purpose of Activity 4 is to allow you to practice the skills necessary to give an oral summary of a discussion, namely, note-taking and preparing the actual summary.

 Activity 4: Note-taking and Summarizing

- Your teacher will divide the class into four groups and ask each group to listen to or read a group discussion.
- Individually, write down the topic and the main ideas.
- Check your notes with a partner in your group and make sure that you both have the same topic and main ideas.

- Next, prepare a summary from your notes. Each person in your group should prepare his or her own summary.
- When writing your summary, you should first decide how you will introduce the topic in your report.
- Then, order the main points made by the participants, and decide which language to use in presenting them.
- Finally, decide what conclusion was reached and prepare a concluding statement.
- In preparing your report, use the language given on page 121.
- Be prepared to report your summary to a different group of students (Activity 5).

Activity 4: STUDENT A

Dracula:	Okay, so today we need to discuss films. What aspect should we focus on?
Marilyn Monroe:	How about the most important element in filmmaking?
Dracula:	Yes, that sounds fine. After all, I've been the most important element in a few films myself. Is that okay with everybody else?
Alfred Hitchcock:	Yes. Of course. That's fine.
Elvis Presley:	Yeah.
Dracula:	Okay, Marilyn, would you like to begin?
Marilyn Monroe:	Yes. Well, in my opinion it's the acting.
Alfred Hitchcock:	Well, you would think that, wouldn't you! As far as I'm concerned, without a director, actors wouldn't be able to function.
Elvis Presley:	I never needed a director.
Alfred Hitchcock:	Exactly my point!
Dracula:	Well, Elvis, if you don't think direction is the most important part of a film, what is?
Elvis Presley:	For me it's the music. Without music, films are boring.
Marilyn Monroe:	Yes, I agree. Don't you think so too, Alfie?
Alfred Hitchcock:	Yes, I do, but don't you think the way the director uses it is more important? For example, the way I use it to build suspense in my films.
Dracula:	I see your point. I wouldn't have been half as frightening without all that music.
Marilyn Monroe:	And I wouldn't have been half as frightened!
Dracula:	Okay, so we all agree. Music, or the way it's used by the director is most important.

Activity 4: STUDENT B

Superman:	Okay, so today we need to discuss crime. What aspect should we focus on?
Sherlock Holmes:	How about the best way to catch a criminal? That's my specialty, you know.
Robin Hood:	Yes, that's a very interesting topic. 5
Catwoman:	Yes, it's fine with me too.
Superman:	Okay, Sherlock, would you like to begin?
Sherlock Holmes:	Yes, certainly. It's a proven scientific fact that the use of logic is the only effective way to catch criminals.
Robin Hood:	Well, it didn't work with me. The Sheriff of Nottingham knew logi- 10 cally where I was, but he couldn't catch me.
Superman:	Yes, that's true. However, I could have caught you by flying into Sherwood Forest. I think using superhuman abilities is the only sure way to catch criminals.
Catwoman:	Is all that really necessary? I've found that feline charm is all you 15 need to catch even the cleverest criminal.
Sherlock Holmes:	Yes, but your methods could hardly be considered serious or efficient; you only work at night. Catching them on a regular basis requires something more.
Superman:	That's what I've been saying. It requires superhuman abilities. 20
Robin Hood:	I agree. You might be able to catch me, Superman, but Mr. Holmes never would.
Sherlock Holmes:	Maybe not, but I would have known exactly what crimes you committed and how you committed them.
Superman:	So, we agree that logic is useful in detecting criminals, but superhu- 25 man abilities are necessary for catching them.

Activity 4: STUDENT C

Benjamin Franklin:	Okay, so today we need to discuss inventions and discoveries. What aspect should we focus on?
Thomas Edison:	How about deciding on the most important invention or discovery of all time?
Alexander Graham Bell:	Okay, that's fine with me.
Mrs. Cheddar:	Yes, that's a good idea. I'd like to suggest the cheese grater. It's made life so much easier for chefs and housewives all around the world.
Thomas Edison:	That's very interesting, Mrs. Cheddar, but it's hardly as important as the electric lightbulb. Just the other day, I had a call from the President of the United States to say how much he's enjoying my invention.
Alexander Graham Bell:	That may be true, but it would be difficult to have a conversation with someone so far away without a telephone, wouldn't it?
Mrs. Cheddar:	Yes, I agree. Perhaps the telephone is more important than my cheese grater. However, lightbulbs may not be completely necessary because, for much of the day, we can get enough sunlight to grate cheese.
Benjamin Franklin:	Yes, but you all have to realize that without my work on electricity, none of your inventions would have been possible.
Mrs. Cheddar:	That's not quite true. You don't need electricity to use a cheese grater! However, I must admit that electricity might be more significant.
Alexander Graham Bell:	Yes, it certainly was essential for my work.
Thomas Edison:	Yes, for mine too.
Benjamin Franklin:	So, we all agree that the most important invention or discovery was the harnessing of electricity.

Activity 4: STUDENT D

Shakespeare:	So, today we need to discuss art. What aspect should we focus on?
Mozart:	What about the purpose of art? That's an interesting topic.
Picasso:	Yes, the purpose of art. What do you think, Your Majesty?
The Queen:	I think it's an excellent topic. It seems to me that the purpose of art is to collect it.
Mozart:	Yes, I see what you mean, but I'm not sure that that's why most people create art. Art provides a way for people to relax. If we listen to a beautiful piece of music, for example, we can forget our daily worries.
Shakespeare:	Yes, that's true, but art also provides us with a chance to laugh and cry. Through art we can experience different emotions in a very short period of time, through plays, for example.
Picasso:	Yes, you have a point, but don't you think that through art we can experiment with different shapes and sizes.
The Queen:	Yes, I was able to collect works of all shapes and sizes!
Picasso:	No, that's not what I meant. I was trying to say that art is about experimenting to find oneself.
Mozart:	Well, I think that all of the points that have been made so far are quite good. Perhaps the purpose of art is a combination of all of them.
Picasso:	I agree.
The Queen:	Yes, so do I.
Shakespeare:	Yes, I agree too. So, to sum up, we all agree that the purpose of art is for relaxation, for experiencing emotions, and for finding oneself . . . and to collect!

CHAPTER ASSIGNMENT: REPORTING ON A GROUP DISCUSSION

 Activity 5: Reporting

For Activity 5 you will present to another group of students the summary that you prepared in Activity 4.

- Your teacher will ask you to form a group with two or three other students who have summarized different dialogues. Each of you will present your summary to the group.
- While the presenter is speaking, he or she will be evaluated by another group member. Before you begin, review the Speaker Evaluation Form below to make sure that everyone in your group understands what will be evaluated. Then decide who will evaluate whom, so that each speaker is evaluated by a different group member.
- At the end of each summary, allow a few minutes for other group members to ask questions about the content of the summary.
- Finally, provide feedback by reviewing the Speaker Evaluation Form with the speaker.

- Remember to use the key language learned in this chapter.

Speaker Evaluation Form

Name of Speaker: _____ *Name of Evaluator:* _____

Topic: _____

Put a ✓+, a ✓, or a ✓– next to each of the following tasks.

The speaker:

_____ was brief.

_____ included only those ideas that were discussed by the group.

_____ included the most important information only.

_____ excluded information that might embarrass a group member.

_____ used appropriate expressions for reporting information to a group:

   _____ Introducing a Topic

   _____ Reporting Opinions

   _____ Concluding a Report

CHAPTER NINE: *Summary of Key Language*

INTRODUCING A TOPIC

On the topic of _____ we . . .

On the subject of _____ we . . .

In our discussion we talked about . . .

We were trying to decide . . .

We discussed . . .

REPORTING OPINIONS

[name] thought that . . .

[name] argued that . . .

[name] added that . . .

[name] suggested that . . .

[name] put forward the idea that . . .

This was supported by [name]

CONCLUDING A REPORT

We came to the conclusion that . . .

We decided that . . .

Thank you.

OTHER

UNIT ASSIGNMENT: THE GROUP DISCUSSION

In this unit you have learned to participate in a group discussion, act as a group leader, and report the main ideas of a discussion to the class. This unit assignment brings together these three skills in a more realistic setting.

- Below is a list of issues. As a class, add some others that interest you.
- Choose the three that interest you the most, and mark them in order of preference. (1 = the most interesting)

    _____ Traveling Abroad: Benefits and Problems
    _____ Technology: Its Role in the Future
    _____ Euthanasia: Who Decides?
    _____ The Death Penalty: The Pros and Cons
    _____ Abortion: A Woman's Right to Choose

    ____ _____
    ____ _____
    ____ _____
    ____ _____
    ____ _____

- Next, mix with the other students in the class and try to find at least two other people who have the same first choice as you. If this is not possible, try to find students who have another of your choices.
- When you have found other students with a similar interest, form a group of four or five, sit down, and choose a group leader and secretary.

- In your small groups you will have five minutes to decide on the focus of the discussion.
- Try to decide on **at least one** main question or problem that needs answering, and then begin your discussion.
- In your discussion, try to reach a decision on the questions or problems that you formulated.
- After you have finished your discussion, your secretary will be asked to report the main points of your discussion to the rest of the class.

- **Remember to use the key language you've learned throughout this unit.**

UNIT 5
THE PEER TUTORIAL

UNIT OUTLINE

Chapter Ten: **GETTING ADVICE**

    Introduction
    Dialogue Analysis
    Practice 1: Asking for Advice
    Practice 2: Giving Advice
    Chapter Assignment 1: Professional Advice
    Chapter Assignment 2: The Peer Tutorial
    Summary of Key Language

UNIT ASSIGNMENT: The Peer Tutorial

Chapter Ten

Getting Advice

INTRODUCTION

A peer tutorial is a meeting in which students exchange ideas or advise each other on their work. It may be an in-class activity or a homework assignment. In writing classes, for example, students may be asked to read and give advice on other students' essays. In a business class, students may be asked to meet outside of class to solve a problem that has been assigned. More informally, students may hold peer tutorials to prepare for an examination.

Successful participation in a peer tutorial is important because it provides an opportunity for students to learn useful information and receive valuable feedback from each other. The discussion skills learned in Chapter Seven as well as the language for requesting and giving advice presented in this unit will help you communicate more effectively in a peer tutorial.

Activity 1: Brainstorming

1. You are planning a trip to a foreign country during your summer vacation. Before you go, you want to get some advice on what to take. Fortunately, one of your classmates is from that country. What expressions would you use to ask for advice?

2. Your classmate is planning a trip to your country and has just asked your advice on what to take. What expressions would you use to give advice?

 **DIALOGUE ANALYSIS**

Listen to the following dialogue once for a general understanding.
Then listen again and complete the highlighting activity below.

Situation: Mike is the host of a call-in radio talk show called What's Your Problem? *Each week he invites an "expert" to help him answer questions on a particular subject. This week the expert's name is Robin U. Daley.*

Mike:	Good evening and welcome to another edition of *What's Your Problem?*, the radio program that answers listeners' questions on any subject they choose. Our "expert" tonight is that infamous master criminal, Robin U. Daley. Good to have you with us, Robin.
Robin:	Nice to be here, Mike.
Mike:	Well, without further ado let's have our first question, which comes from Mrs. Needy of Michigan. Hello. You're on the air.
Mrs. Needy:	Yes . . . Hello. I'd like to make a lot of money as quickly as possible. What do you think I should do, Robin?
Robin:	Well, if I were you I'd steal it. It's what I do, and I've always found it very reward-ing. To begin with, you might try burglary. It's an easy way to start because you can work by yourself, the equipment you need isn't very expensive and, above all, the general public cooperates by leaving windows open all the time.
Mrs. Needy:	The general idea of stealing sounds good, but I'm not sure about burglary. I don't think my husband would like me working nights. What else do you suggest I do?
Robin:	Well, if you don't like night work, have you ever thought about robbing banks? It might be a little bit more difficult than burglary, but they're open during the day, so your husband shouldn't mind. If you do choose to rob banks, it might be a good idea to wear a disguise, and you may want to employ an assistant to drive the get-away car. Both of these will increase your costs, but you should be able to get a good return on your investment if you choose the right bank at the right time.
Mrs. Needy:	That sounds like a good idea. Which bank do you recommend?
Robin:	Well, I always rob the National Bank, as it's the most popular one in the country, but I vary the time; sometimes I rob it on Friday morning when everybody has deposited their salary, but last week I robbed it on Monday afternoon, just to keep the police guessing.

5

10

15

20

25

30

ON AIR

Mrs. Needy: Wait a minute! The reason I need to make money is because somebody stole all of mine from the National Bank last Monday afternoon! 35

Robin: Ah, well, erm . . . one final thing I'd recommend if you're going to enter this profession is to get yourself a good lawyer. Goodbye.

Mike: Er, well, er, Robin seems to have left us in rather a hurry, er, so that seems to be the end of this week's show. So, until next 40 week, goodnight.

 ## Activity 2: Highlighting

1. Highlight the three expressions that Mrs. Needy uses *to ask for advice*.
2. Highlight the expressions that Robin uses *to give advice*.

 ## Activity 3: Fluency Circles

PRACTICE 1: ASKING FOR ADVICE

The purpose of Activity 3 is to practice asking for advice.

- Your teacher will give each of you a strip of paper with a statement on it.
- Read the statement and try to remember it.
- Then, your teacher will ask you and your classmates to form two circles, one inside the other.
- With your first partner, state the idea on your strip of paper and then use one of the expressions to ask for advice.
- After you and your partner have both asked for advice, your teacher will ask you to move on to a new partner.
- Repeat the activity until your teacher tells you to stop.
- Try using all four of the expressions for asking for advice, especially those that you are least familiar with.

Sample Dialogue

A: I think I'm getting a cold, but I have a test this afternoon. **What do you think I should do?**

B: **Why don't you** try resting for a few hours?

A: Yes, that's a good idea. Thanks.

Key Language

Asking for Advice
What do you think I should do?
What do you suggest I do?
What do you recommend I do?
What should I do?

Giving Advice
Why don't you try + (VERB) + ing.

PRACTICE 2: GIVING ADVICE

The purpose of Activity 4 is to practice giving advice.

 Activity 4: Class Mingle

- Your teacher will give you a piece of paper with one problem and three pieces of advice. Write these on the top of the following page in the space provided.
- When you are ready, mix with the other students in the class and try to find three pieces of advice that fit your problem.
- When you are given advice that fits, write it and the name of the student in the space provided. (If you are given advice that does not fit, make a strange face to show that it doesn't make sense.)
- When other students ask you for advice, you should give them only the advice written on your page.
- Remember to use the key language you learned in Activity 3 as well as the language printed on the bottom of the following page.
- **Try to give advice in as many ways as you can.**

Sample Dialogue 1

A: Excuse me. I've lost my textbook. What do you think I should do?

B: If I were you, I'd call a doctor.

A: (Makes a funny face.) Thanks.

Sample Dialogue 2

A: Excuse me. I've lost my textbook. What do you recommend I do?

B: It might be a good idea to tell your teacher.

A: Yes, that's a good idea. Thanks. Let me write down your name. (Writes down name and advice.)

Activity 4: Worksheet

Problem:

Advice:

Name	Advice

Key Language

Asking for Advice	*Giving Advice*
What do you think I should do?	I always . . .
What do you suggest I do?	Sometimes I . . .
What do you recommend I do?	If I were you, I'd . . .
What should I do?	How about . . . ?
	You might try . . .
	You may want to . . .
	Maybe you could . . .
	It might be a good idea to . . .
	Have you ever thought about . . . ?
	One thing I'd recommend is . . .
	Another thing I'd recommend is . . .

CHAPTER ASSIGNMENT 1: PROFESSIONAL ADVICE

 Activity 5: Role Play

Anytown, U.S.A. has an advice hotline, which is a service that helps people solve their problems. People from the town call up, describe their problems, and ask for advice.

- Your teacher will ask each member of your group to turn to a different page in your book.
- With the other two or three people in your group, act out the roles described on that page.
- For each role play, one person will play the role of the advice counselor, and one will act as the advice seeker. The third person in your group will evaluate the role of the advice counselor by using the evaluation form below.
- **Remember to use the key language that you have just learned.**

Professional Advice: Speaker Evaluation Form

Evaluator: _____   *Advice Counselor:* _____

Listen and observe the student who is playing the role of the advice counselor.
Put a ✓ next to each of the expressions you hear.

Giving Advice

_____ I always . . .   _____ Maybe you could . . .
_____ Sometimes I . . .   _____ It might be a good idea to . . .
_____ If I were you, I'd . . .   _____ Have you ever thought about . . . ?
_____ How about . . . ?   _____ One thing I'd recommend is . . .
_____ You might try . . .   _____ Another thing I'd recommend is . . .
_____ You may want to . . .

COMMENTS:

Activity 5: Role Play   **STUDENT A**

Activity 5 consists of three role plays. In the first role play you will play an advice counselor, in the second you will play an advice seeker, and in the third you will be the evaluator. Try to do the role plays without looking at the key language on the right side of the page. If you finish before the other groups, switch role sheets and begin again.

ROLE ONE: ADVICE COUNSELOR

You are an advice counselor. You work for an advice hotline, a service that helps people solve their problems. You are about to receive a telephone call from someone who needs your advice. Answer the telephone, listen to the problem, and give that person advice. You may answer the phone by saying,

"Advice Hotline, this is (name) speaking. May I help you?"

• **Remember to use the appropriate expressions for giving advice.**

KEY LANGUAGE:

Giving Advice
I always . . .
Sometimes I . . .
If I were you, I'd . . .
How about . . . ?
You might try . . .
You may want to . . .
Maybe you could . . .
It might be a good idea to . . .
Have you ever thought about . . . ?
One thing I'd recommend is . . .
Another thing I'd recommend is . . .

ROLE TWO: ADVICE SEEKER

A woman in your neighborhood watches everything from her window. She watches when you enter or leave your house. She loves to spread gossip about what she sees. You wish she would mind her own business. Call the advice hotline and ask for advice.

KEY LANGUAGE:

Asking for Advice
What do you think I should do?
What do you suggest I do?
What do you recommend I do?
What should I do?

ROLE THREE: EVALUATOR

You are the evaluator. Using the evaluation form on page 138, evaluate the student playing the role of ADVICE COUNSELOR.

Activity 5: Role Play   **STUDENT B**

Activity 5 consists of three role plays. In the first role play you will be the evaluator, in the second you will play an advice counselor, and in the third you will play an advice seeker. Try to do the role plays without looking at the key language on the right side of the page. If you finish before the other groups, switch role sheets and begin again.

ROLE ONE: EVALUATOR

You are the evaluator. Using the evaluation form on page 138, evaluate the student playing the role of ADVICE COUNSELOR.

ROLE TWO: ADVICE COUNSELOR

You are an advice counselor. You work for an advice hotline, a service that helps people solve their problems. You are about to receive a telephone call from someone who needs your advice. Answer the telephone, listen to the problem, and give that person advice. You may answer the phone by saying,

"Advice Hotline, this is (name) speaking. May I help you?

• Remember to use the appropriate expressions for giving advice.

KEY LANGUAGE:

Giving Advice
I always . . .
Sometimes I . . .
If I were you, I'd . . .
How about . . . ?
You might try . . .
You may want to . . .
Maybe you could . . .
It might be a good idea to . . .
Have you ever thought about . . . ?
One thing I'd recommend is . . .
Another thing I'd recommend is . . .

ROLE THREE: ADVICE SEEKER

You have a friend who you like very much. However, you have just realized that he never tells the truth. You want to continue the friendship, but you don't like being lied to. Call the advice hotline and ask for advice.

KEY LANGUAGE:

Asking for Advice
What do you think I should do?
What do you suggest I do?
What do you recommend I do?
What should I do?

Activity 5: Role Play STUDENT C

Activity 5 consists of three role plays. In the first role play you will play an advice seeker, in the second you will be the evaluator, and in the third you will play an advice counselor. Try to do the role plays without looking at the key language on the right side of the page. If you finish before the other groups, switch role sheets and begin again.

ROLE ONE: ADVICE SEEKER	
One of your classmates is very lazy. He is often absent from class and when he does attend, he sleeps. When he is absent, he calls you and asks to photocopy your notes. You are tired of doing his work for him. Call the advice hotline and ask for advice.	KEY LANGUAGE: *Asking for Advice* What do you think I should do? What do you suggest I do? What do you recommend I do? What should I do?

ROLE TWO: EVALUATOR	
You are the evaluator. Using the evaluation form on page 138, evaluate the student playing the role of ADVICE COUNSELOR.	

ROLE THREE: ADVICE COUNSELOR	
You are an advice counselor. You work for an advice hotline, a service that helps people solve their problems. You are about to receive a telephone call from someone who needs your advice. Answer the telephone, listen to the problem, and give that person advice. You may answer the phone by saying, "Advice Hotline, this is (name) speaking. May I help you? • **Remember to use the appropriate expressions for giving advice.**	KEY LANGUAGE: *Giving Advice* I always . . . Sometimes I . . . If I were you, I'd . . . How about . . . ? You might try . . . You may want to . . . Maybe you could . . . It might be a good idea to . . . Have you ever thought about . . . ? One thing I'd recommend is . . . Another thing I'd recommend is . . .

CHAPTER ASSIGNMENT 2: THE PEER TUTORIAL

 Activity 6: Role Play

STUDENT A

With your partner, role play the following situations, using all of the language that you have practiced in this chapter.

Role Play One

Your writing teacher assigned you to write an essay for today's class and to participate in a peer tutorial with another student. The purpose of the tutorial is to give advice on each other's essays. Your partner has just finished reading your essay. Ask for advice.

Role Play Two

Your writing teacher assigned you to write an essay for today's class and to participate in a peer tutorial with another student. The purpose of the tutorial is to give advice on each other's essays. Your partner will begin by asking you for advice. Please give advice on the following points:

> The essay was very well-focused.
> The conclusion was a little bit weak.
> The ideas were not presented in the most convincing order.
> Some of the examples were unclear.
> Your partner forgot to give the essay a title.
> Other?

Role Play Three

You and a classmate have been assigned to give a presentation in class tomorrow. You have finished preparing it and practicing it together. Now it is time for you to advise each other on what changes to make. Your partner will begin by asking you for advice. Please give advice on the following points:

> It was interesting.
> The ideas were not very well organized.
> The delivery was not very effective.
> The eye contact was not very good.
> Your partner spoke too fast.
> Your partner spoke too quietly.
> Other?

Role Play Four

You and a classmate have been assigned to give a presentation in class tomorrow. You have finished preparing it and practicing it together. Now it is time for you to advise each other on what changes to make. Ask your partner to advise you on your part of the presentation.

CHAPTER ASSIGNMENT 2: THE PEER TUTORIAL

 Activity 6: Role Play

STUDENT B

With your partner, role play the following situations, using all of the language that you have practiced in this chapter.

Role Play One

Your writing teacher assigned you to write an essay for today's class and to participate in a peer tutorial with another student. The purpose of the tutorial is to give advice on each other's essays. You have just finished reading your partner's essay. Your partner will begin by asking you for advice. Please give advice on the following points:

The topic was extremely interesting.
Some of the sentences were unclear.
The essay lacked strong transitions.
The introduction wasn't very interesting.
Your partner misspelled a lot of words.
Other?

Role Play Two

Your writing teacher assigned you to write an essay for today's class and to participate in a peer tutorial with another student. The purpose of the tutorial is to give advice on each other's essays. Please begin the role play by asking your partner for advice on your essay.

Role Play Three

You and a classmate have been assigned to give a presentation in class tomorrow. You have finished preparing it and practicing it together. Now it is time for you to advise each other on what changes to make. Begin the role play by asking your partner to advise you on your part of the presentation.

Role Play Four

You and a classmate have been assigned to give a presentation in class tomorrow. You have finished preparing it and practicing it together. Now it is time for you to advise each other on what changes to make. Your partner will begin by asking for advice. Please give advice on the following points:

It was well-organized.
Your partner did not include enough examples.
The presentation needs stronger transitions.
Some of the words were too difficult to understand.
Your partner forgot to look up at the audience.
Your partner spoke too slowly.
Your partner spoke too loudly.
Other?

CHAPTER TEN: *Summary of Key Language*

ASKING FOR ADVICE

What do you think I should do?
What do you suggest I do?
What do you recommend I do?
What should I do?

GIVING ADVICE

I always . . .
Sometimes I . . .
If I were you, I'd . . .
How about . . . ?
You might try . . .
You may want to . . .
Maybe you could . . .
It might be a good idea to . . .
Have you ever thought about . . . ?
One thing I'd recommend is . . .
Another thing I'd recommend is . . .

OTHER

UNIT ASSIGNMENT: THE PEER TUTORIAL

Rather than doing the Unit Assignment now, we will do it at the end of the next chapter, Chapter Eleven, when you are working on a project that you will need feedback on. You will get more information on this assignment at that time, but for now, here's an overview:

In Chapter Eleven, you will be asked to give an information presentation to a small group of your peers. Before giving your "real" presentation, you will give a "practice" presentation in front of a different group. One member of this group will evaluate your presentation and give you feedback so that you can make improvements before giving it in front of your "real" audience. You will also give that student feedback on his or her presentation. This exchange of information will serve as the peer tutorial for the unit assignment for this chapter.

UNIT 6

Presentations

Chapter Eleven: **PRESENTING INFORMATION TO A SMALL GROUP**

Introduction
Dialogue Analysis
Practice 1: Choosing a Topic
Practice 2: Preparing the Introduction
Practice 3: Preparing the Body
Practice 4: Preparing the Conclusion
Practice 5: Preparing Note Cards
Practice 6: Questioning a Speaker
Practice 7: Practicing Your Presentation
Chapter Assignment: Presenting Information to a Small
    Group
Summary of Key Language

Chapter Twelve: **DEMONSTRATING A PROCESS TO A GROUP**

Introduction
Dialogue Analysis
Practice 1: Choosing a Topic
Practice 2: Using Visual Aids
Practice 3: Describing a Process
Practice 4: Reminding Someone to Do Something
Chapter Assignment: Demonstrating a Process to a Group
Summary of Key Language

Chapter Thirteen: **PLANNING A GROUP PROJECT**

Introduction
Dialogue Analysis
Practice 1: Making Suggestions
Practice 2: Volunteering to Help
Practice 3: Asking for Volunteers
Chapter Assignment: Planning a Group Project
Summary of Key Language

UNIT ASSIGNMENT: The Group Project

Chapter Eleven

Presenting Information to a Small Group

INTRODUCTION

Education takes place through an exchange of ideas, not only between teachers and students, but also among students themselves. Thus, instructors provide opportunities in class for students to exchange ideas on various topics. Sometime during your academic career, you will be expected to present information to others, either formally, informally, or both. Formally, you may be required to present your ideas or the ideas of others to an entire class. Informally, you may be assigned to report information to a small group of three or four students. No matter how informal the presentation, you will be expected to present your ideas clearly and logically.

Step-by-step preparation will help you present your ideas clearly:

* Choose an appropriate topic for your specific audience
* Understand why you are presenting your ideas (What is your purpose?)
* Organize your ideas carefully
* Prepare sufficiently
* Deliver your ideas effectively

 Activity 1: Pairwork Discussion

1. Have you ever given a presentation, either in English or in your native language? If so, how did you feel? If not, what do you imagine the experience is like?

2. How do you feel about giving a presentation in this class?

DIALOGUE ANALYSIS

 Activity 2: Listening

Listen to the student presentation on scuba diving and, using the note-taking sheet provided below, take notes on the main points.

Situation: A student is giving an information presentation to a small group of students.

Some Possible Dangers of Scuba Diving

Introduction

    S:

    C:

    U:

    B:

    A:

Body

  First category of danger:

    Type 1:

    Type 2:

    Type 3:

  Next category of danger:

    Type 1:

    Type 2:

  Last category of danger:

    Example 1:

    Example 2:

    Example 3:

    Example 4:

    Example 5:

    Example 6:

Conclusion

  Advice for avoiding danger:

Some Possible Dangers of Scuba Diving

[Introduction]

Raise your hand if you've been scuba diving before. Do any of you have friends who have been diving? Do you know what SCUBA means? No? SCUBA means "Self Contained Underwater Breathing Apparatus." In other words, scuba diving means being able to breathe under the water with a "breathing machine." Traditionally, scuba diving was done for professional 5 reasons, for example, to build tunnels, to repair boats, and for scientific research. Later, however, people started diving for recreation, which we now call "sport diving." In other words, people started diving for enjoyment, so that they could be active in the water and experience a sense of weightlessness. They enjoy the beauty found in 10 the ocean, and they enjoy being in an environment where they are constantly learning new things. However, along with the pleasures come many dangers that all divers should be aware of. So, today I'd like to talk about three 15 different categories of danger that divers may encounter under the water: physical dangers, ocean dangers, and animal dangers.

[Body]

The first category I'd like to talk about 20 is the physical dangers of scuba diving, and the three types that I'd like to look at today are the bends, air embolism, and nitrogen narcosis. The first type is the bends. The bends is probably the most famous scuba diving danger because it's been popularized in movies. The 25 bends is caused by diving for too long a period of time at a particular depth. When a diver dives too long, air bubbles form in the blood and tissues and can cause a variety of symptoms, for instance, blindness, dizziness, paralysis, unconsciousness, choking, rash, or convulsions. The only cure for the bends is to [be] put immediately into a recompression chamber. Inside the chamber, the 30 pressure is slowly reduced so that the size of the nitrogen bubbles are reduced and eventually disappear.

The second type of physical danger is air embolism, or bubbles in your blood. Air embolism occurs when air is breathed in at one depth and breathed out at another depth. In other words, it can occur when a diver holds his or 35 her breath and changes depth. An air embolism can block the flow of blood to the brain, which can cause death. Like the bends, the cure for air embolism is to put the victim into a recompression chamber to gradually change the pressure until it reaches normal surface pressure.

The third type of physical danger is nitrogen narcosis, and the cause of 40 nitrogen narcosis is diving too deep. When divers dive too deep, they begin to lose their sense of perception and muscle coordination, and may become dizzy. Sometimes a diver believes that it is possible to breathe underwater, so he takes off his equipment and drowns. The cure for nitrogen narcosis is for the diver to move to a shallower depth. This will cause some of the nitrogen 45 to leave the body.

The next category of danger that I'd like to talk about is ocean danger, and I'll talk about two types today: currents and waves. Currents are like rivers in the ocean. They can be dangerous because they can be very strong and can drag a diver out to sea. This can be especially dangerous if a diver is 50 diving from shore and is dragged away from the group. Another problem is that divers may find themselves swimming against a current, which can cause them to become extremely tired. Waves are a problem when a diver is entering or leaving the water. Along the shore, waves may knock a diver down and cause injury. Or they may cause a diver to become seasick either in the water 55 or on a bouncing boat.

The last category of danger is animal danger, and today I'd like to give you six examples of animals that pose a danger to humans. The most famous example of these, of course, is the shark. We've all heard of "man-eating sharks." But one thing to remember is that there are many different types of 60 sharks, and each type of shark tends to live only in certain areas. So, before diving, find out whether there are sharks, what kinds of sharks there are, and whether or not they are harmful to divers. Most sharks, in fact, don't bother divers. Another example of a fish which has a reputation for attacking divers is the barracuda, which has sharp, visible teeth and can attack quickly. 65 However, barracudas are more interested in attacking fish and rarely attack divers. Some fish that do pose a real danger to divers are poisonous bottom-dwelling fish, for instance, the stonefish and the stingray. These fish will not attack divers, but will inject poison if they are accidentally stepped on. So divers must be careful of where they walk and kneel. A similar example is the 70 sea urchin, which has long spines which, if accidentally touched, can stick into the diver's skin. The last example that I'd like to mention today is coral, which you may find surprising. Although coral is one of the most beautiful animals in the ocean, many divers have cut themselves on sharp coral, which takes a very long time to heal. Also, one type of coral, called "fire coral" is 75 poisonous and causes the skin to sting and itch.

[Conclusion]

In conclusion, I'd like to emphasize that scuba diving is fun and not too dangerous as long as you prepare carefully. Some ways to avoid danger are to take a certified course by a licensed instructor before you dive, and never dive alone. Also, be sure to check the conditions of the water before you enter. 80 Make sure that you are familiar with the ocean and wildlife in the area where you plan to dive. In addition, a good diver always dives according to an agreed-upon plan and makes sure that all equipment is in good working condition and has been well maintained. All of these will ensure that you have a very pleasurable and safe diving experience. 85

Thank you. Do you have any questions?

Student One:	I'm sorry, but I didn't quite understand what you meant by a recompression chamber. Could you explain it again, please?
Presenter:	Yes. A recompression chamber is a like a small room. A diver is placed in the room and the pressure can be changed so that 90 the diver's body can adjust more slowly and return to normal.
Student One:	Thank you.
Student Two:	In your presentation you used the word "embolism." Could you spell that, please?
Presenter:	Certainly. It's E - M - B - O - L - I - S - M. 95
Student Two:	Thanks.
Student Two:	Could you please repeat what you said about stingrays?
Presenter:	Yes. Stingrays live on the bottom of the ocean and have a sharp spine on their tails. In general, they won't bother divers, but if a diver steps on the tail of a stingray, the 100 stingray may inject poison, so divers need to be careful that they don't step or kneel on them.
Student Two:	Have you ever stepped on one?
Presenter:	No. Not yet. Yes?
Student Three:	In your presentation you mentioned that there are many types 105 of sharks. I was wondering if you could give us an example.
Presenter:	Yes. One of the most dangerous sharks is the great white shark, which, in addition to living off other coasts of the world, lives off the coast of California. There are also less dangerous sharks, such as sand sharks. Okay, well if there are 110 no more questions, I hope you enjoyed the presentation. Thank you for listening.

Activity 3: Highlighting

1. Highlight the expression that the presenter uses to *introduce the topic.*
2. Highlight the different expressions that the presenter uses to *order information.*
3. Highlight the different expressions that the presenter uses to *give examples.*
4. Highlight the expression that the presenter uses to *conclude the presentation.*
5. Highlight *the final question* that the presenter uses.
6. Highlight *the four expressions* that the members of the audience use to *ask questions* at the end of the presentation.
7. What is the speaker's purpose? (to persuade? to inform? to demonstrate? to move the audience?)

Activity 4: Small Group Discussion

PRACTICE 1: CHOOSING A TOPIC

The purpose of Activity 4 is to teach you how to choose an appropriate topic for an information presentation.

The first step in preparing your presentation is to choose a topic that is
- interesting for you and your audience
- appropriate

Choose an Interesting Topic

Your topic should be one that is interesting to you and to your classmates. If you are interested in the topic, then you will be enthusiastic when you speak. If your audience is interested in your topic, then they will enjoy and learn from your presentation, rather than grow bored and fall asleep. Depending on your assignment, your topic may be one with which you are already very familiar, or it may be a topic that you will need to research. In both cases, you will need to choose a topic about which you have, or can easily get, information.

Choose an Appropriate Topic

Make sure that the topic you choose is appropriate for the length of time that you will be required to speak. This means that your topic should not be too general or too specific for the amount of time allotted. Additionally, you should not choose a topic that is too technical or too simple for your audience. Choose a topic that is both understandable and yet not too obvious. Finally, try not to choose a topic that will make your audience uncomfortable.

Activity 4: Worksheet

At the end of this chapter, you will be asked to give a five- to ten-minute information presentation to a small audience of two or three students. The purpose of this information presentation is to provide information about a specific topic of your choice.

1. The following is a list of possible presentation topics. First, discuss each topic with the other students in your group, and put an 'X' in the appropriate box if that particular topic does not meet the given criteria. Remember that you are looking for topics that would be appropriate for **a five- to ten-minute information presentation.**

	Interesting? (Not too obvious)	Specific Enough?	Appropriate Content?	Easily Understood?
What I Ate for Breakfast				
Some Benefits of Regular Exercise				
Wildlife in Australia				
Dangers of Riding a Motorcycle				
The Joys of Camping				
The Beginning of the Universe				

2. Next, look at the chart that you have just filled in and choose the two topics that your group felt had the most problems. Decide whether it is possible to adapt the topics to make them appropriate. How would you do this?

1. _____

2. _____

3. Finally, choose the two topics that your group felt were the most appropriate and brainstorm possible points that might be covered in the presentation.

Topic 1: _____

Main Points:

Topic 2: _____

Main Points:

Activity 5: Small Group Discussion

The purpose of Activity 5 is to help you choose an appropriate topic for your information presentation.

Now think of three other possible topics for your information presentation, and list them below. Then, discuss each one with your partners, using the grid from Activity 4.

1. _____

2. _____

3. _____

When preparing your presentation, it is very important that you spend time planning your introduction because the introduction will set the tone for the rest of your presentation. If your introduction is interesting, then your audience will be more likely to pay close attention to what you are saying. If your introduction is disorganized or boring, the members of your audience may lose interest. The following information will help you prepare an effective introduction.

The Purpose of the Introduction

The introduction of your presentation should:

1. attract the attention of your audience and establish rapport
2. state your topic clearly

1. Attention-getters

Speakers use several "techniques" for attracting the attention of the audience. In planning your own presentation, try to use some of the following:

- Provide background information

  Providing background information is an excellent opportunity to give your audience general information about your topic. You may want to provide a short description or brief history of the subject.

- Ask a question

  Asking a question will give the audience a moment to think about some aspect of your topic. It is important, however, if you choose this technique, that you choose your question carefully. You may want to say, for example, "Raise your hand if you have ever . . . " rather than "Has anybody ever . . .?" It's easier to raise a hand than to answer a question verbally so, by phrasing the question in this way, you may get a bigger response from your audience.

- Include a short quotation

  Including a quotation in your introduction can add credibility to your presentation. For example, if you were giving a presentation on nutrition, you may want to begin with a short quotation from a famous nutritionist. This will show your audience that "experts" also share your opinions, and may make your presentation seem more valuable or important to them.

- Tell a short story

  Sometimes it is effective to describe a problem by describing the life of a person who suffers from that problem. For example, if you were giving a presentation on "Discrimination Against AIDS Patients," in your introduction you may want to briefly describe the lifestyle of one AIDS patient. Then, draw a connection between the experience of this one person and how that problem affects a large number of people. This technique helps to personalize the topic for the audience.

PRACTICE 2: PREPARING THE INTRODUCTION

The purpose of Activity 6 is to learn how to identify the parts of an introduction in preparation for writing the introduction for your own presentation.

2. Stating your topic clearly

It is essential that you state your topic clearly in the introduction. The best place to do this is at the end of the introduction as a signal to the audience that the introduction of the presentation has finished and that the main body of the presentation is about to begin. You may also want to include a "presentation plan" that highlights for the audience what the main topics of the presentation will be.

 Activity 6: Small Group Discussion

1. Look again at the speech on pages 151-153. What technique(s) does the speaker use to attract the attention of the audience?

2. What expression does the speaker use to introduce the topic of the presentation?

3. Does the speaker include a presentation plan? If so, what is it?

4. Look at the three possible topics that you chose in Activity 5 for your information presentation. What technique(s) do you think would attract the attention of your audience?

5. For each of the three topics you chose in Activity 5, write a complete sentence that you could use in your introduction to state your topic to the audience.

Once you have prepared an effective introduction, especially if you have included a presentation plan, then the body of your essay should follow logically from it. In other words, if you have said that you are going to talk about x, y, and z, then you should talk about x, y, and z!

Furthermore, it is essential that the main points of your presentation are supported by clear examples that will be easily understood by your audience. The number of examples you choose will vary depending on the point you are making. However, it is important to remember that each point must be adequately supported.

 **Activity 7: Groupwork**

Choose **one** of the three topics that you listed in Activity 5. Working in pairs or groups of three, fill in the following outline by brainstorming *three main points* and *two possible examples* that you might include in a presentation on this topic.

Topic: _____

  First main point: _____

    First example: _____

    Second example: _____

  Second main point: _____

    First example: _____

    Second example: _____

  Third main point: _____

    First example: _____

    Second example: _____

PRACTICE 3: PREPARING THE BODY

The purpose of Activity 7 is to learn how to prepare the body of a presentation.

PRACTICE 4: PREPARING THE CONCLUSION

The purpose of Activity 8 is to help you identify effective presentation conclusions in preparation for writing the conclusion to your information presentation.

The purpose of the conclusion is to sum up your main points and/or offer a final thought on the topic. The conclusion generally has two parts:

1. a restatement of the topic
2. a final thought

1. Restating the Topic

The restatement of the topic is a sentence or two in which you restate the main idea of the presentation. This does not mean that you simply repeat what you have said at the end of your introduction, but that you offer the same ideas, using different words. In other words, the first sentence of your conclusion should have approximately the same meaning as the topic stated in the introduction, but should be stated using different vocabulary and grammar.

2. Offering a Final Thought

For the final thought of the presentation, you may want to offer advice to your listeners, provide a solution to a problem that you have discussed, or make a prediction for the future. You may also want to talk briefly about your own personal experience or make a call for action. Depending on your topic and purpose, you may want to include more than one of these in your conclusion. Remember, this is your last chance to make an impression on your audience!

 **Activity 8: Pairwork**

In pairs, read each of the conclusions below and do the following:

1. Underline the topic of the presentation
2. Decide what technique is used to offer the final thought

     A. giving advice
     B. offering a solution
     C. making a prediction
     D. making a call to action
     E. using personal experience

Remember that more than one technique can be used.

Conclusion #1: The Pleasures of Camping

To sum up, camping can be a very rewarding experience, especially for those people who live in the city. Camping can give us a chance to relax, to see plants and animals in their natural environments, and to escape from the pace of city life. However, it's important to remember that camping can have its problems, especially if you don't have much experience doing it. If you've never been camping before, but are interested in trying it, there are a few ways that you can make your camping trip a safe one. First of all, you may want to consider going with a group, such as a university outdoors club. Secondly, be sure to research the place where you plan to go camping. Find out what, if any, dangerous wildlife may be found there and learn how to protect yourself. Finally, make sure that you have the proper equipment. Good equipment will ensure that your trip is safe and as comfortable as possible. If you follow these guidelines, you too can experience the beauty and peace of the wilderness.

Conclusion #2: The Benefits of Regular Exercise

As I mentioned before, regular exercise will change your life. You will feel better because you will be able to breathe easier and sleep better. And, if you combine regular exercise with a healthy diet, you will probably discover that you become sick less often. A healthy body will also make you feel happier, which may lead to better relations with your family and friends.

Regular exercise sure changed my life. I am generally a happier person, and I find that I can accomplish more in a day. My friends even tell me that I am more fun to be with than I was before!

Don't think of exercise as something you MUST do; think of regular exercise as a way of life, a way of doing something special for yourself, a time to enjoy your body. If you have a positive attitude about exercise, then you will have a positive attitude about your life. Don't wait! Take a positive step. Start exercising today!

Conclusion #3: The Risks of Nuclear Power

In summary, the risks of using nuclear power far outweigh the benefits. First of all, it is becoming more and more difficult to find ways to dispose of nuclear waste. Secondly, the risk of an accident increases as our nuclear power plants age. Finally, many people worry about the possibility of making nuclear weapons from nuclear by-products.

We must stop the use of nuclear power in the world. It's time for us to discover new, clean forms of energy, such as solar energy, and we should fund research in this area. We need to contact politicians and tell them how we feel about the risks of nuclear power, and we must tell our friends, neighbors, and family members about the dangers that we are living with. Until we discontinue the use of nuclear power, our planet and our loved ones will never be safe on this earth. Please take action today! Only we can make a difference!

PRACTICE 5: PREPARING NOTE CARDS

The purpose of Activity 9 is to learn how to prepare note cards for use during a presentation.

 Activity 9: Pairwork

With your partner, look at the note cards that follow and answer the following questions:

1. Why has the speaker numbered all of the note cards?

2. What headings has the speaker written on the top of the note cards? Why?

3. How many introduction note cards are there? Body note cards? Conclusion note cards? Why might the speaker have written so many introduction note cards?

4. Has the speaker included delivery cues? Why?

5. How many different techniques has the speaker used to make the cards easy to use? (Think about the number of complete sentences and the general layout of the cards.)

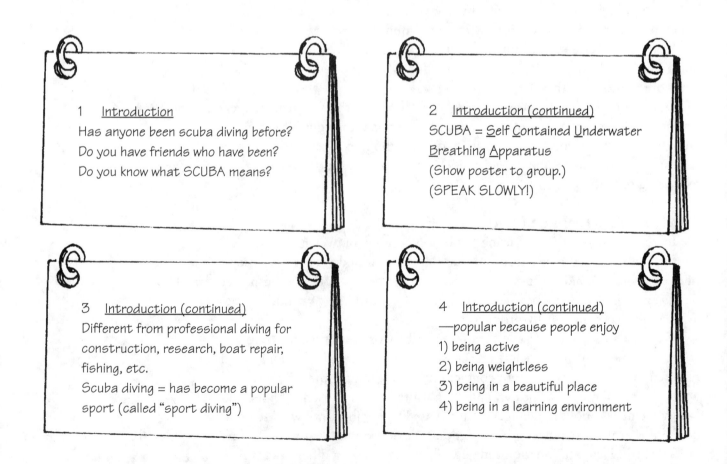

1   Introduction
Has anyone been scuba diving before?
Do you have friends who have been?
Do you know what SCUBA means?

2   Introduction (continued)
SCUBA = <u>S</u>elf <u>C</u>ontained <u>U</u>nderwater
<u>B</u>reathing <u>A</u>pparatus
(Show poster to group.)
(SPEAK SLOWLY!)

3   Introduction (continued)
Different from professional diving for construction, research, boat repair, fishing, etc.
Scuba diving = has become a popular sport (called "sport diving")

4   Introduction (continued)
—popular because people enjoy
1) being active
2) being weightless
3) being in a beautiful place
4) being in a learning environment

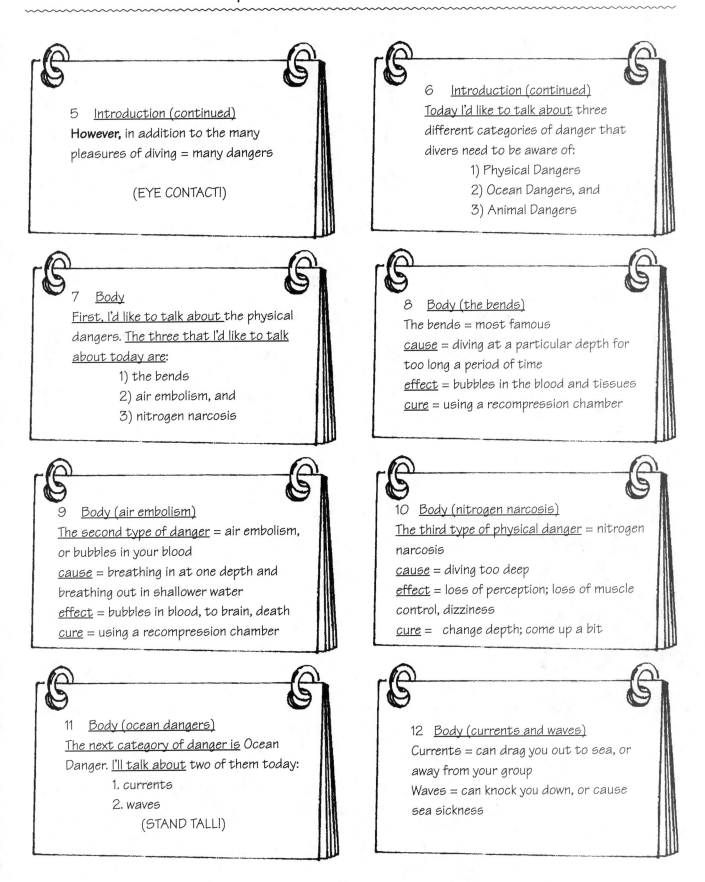

5   Introduction (continued)
However, in addition to the many pleasures of diving = many dangers

(EYE CONTACT!)

6   Introduction (continued)
Today I'd like to talk about three different categories of danger that divers need to be aware of:
    1) Physical Dangers
    2) Ocean Dangers, and
    3) Animal Dangers

7   Body
First, I'd like to talk about the physical dangers. The three that I'd like to talk about today are:
    1) the bends
    2) air embolism, and
    3) nitrogen narcosis

8   Body (the bends)
The bends = most famous
cause = diving at a particular depth for too long a period of time
effect = bubbles in the blood and tissues
cure = using a recompression chamber

9   Body (air embolism)
The second type of danger = air embolism, or bubbles in your blood
cause = breathing in at one depth and breathing out in shallower water
effect = bubbles in blood, to brain, death
cure = using a recompression chamber

10   Body (nitrogen narcosis)
The third type of physical danger = nitrogen narcosis
cause = diving too deep
effect = loss of perception; loss of muscle control, dizziness
cure =   change depth; come up a bit

11   Body (ocean dangers)
The next category of danger is Ocean Danger. I'll talk about two of them today:
    1. currents
    2. waves
        (STAND TALL!)

12   Body (currents and waves)
Currents = can drag you out to sea, or away from your group
Waves = can knock you down, or cause sea sickness

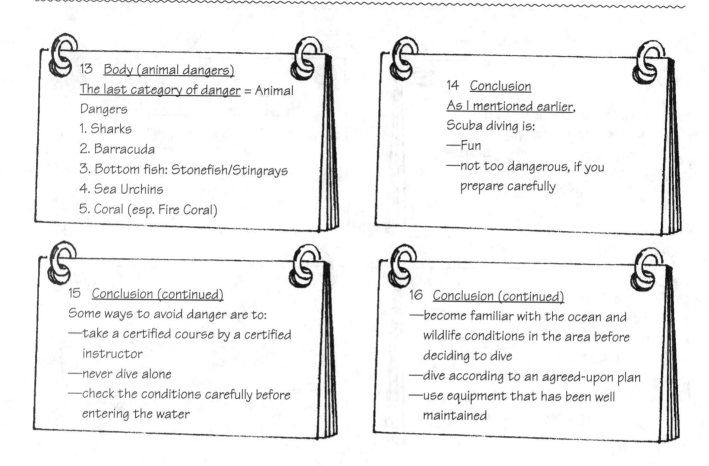

13 <u>Body (animal dangers)</u>
<u>The last category of danger</u> = Animal
Dangers
1. Sharks
2. Barracuda
3. Bottom fish: Stonefish/Stingrays
4. Sea Urchins
5. Coral (esp. Fire Coral)

14 <u>Conclusion</u>
<u>As I mentioned earlier,</u>
Scuba diving is:
—Fun
—not too dangerous, if you
    prepare carefully

15 <u>Conclusion (continued)</u>
Some ways to avoid danger are to:
—take a certified course by a certified
    instructor
—never dive alone
—check the conditions carefully before
    entering the water

16 <u>Conclusion (continued)</u>
—become familiar with the ocean and
    wildlife conditions in the area before
    deciding to dive
—dive according to an agreed-upon plan
—use equipment that has been well
    maintained

PRACTICE 6: QUESTIONING A SPEAKER

The purpose of Activity 10 is to give you practice using expressions to question a speaker.

Activity 10: Class Mingle

- For this activity use the chart on page 166 and the card that your teacher will give you.
- Your card will have five pieces of information written on it: a topic, a sentence that includes an unknown word, a definition, an example, and the spelling of the word. This is the information that you will give your classmates when they ask you for it.
- Write the information on your card in the space provided in the chart.
- Your task is to mix with the other students in the class and to ask for the information you need to complete your chart.

- Before you begin, practice the sample dialogue that follows with a partner.
- When everyone is ready, mix with the other students in the class and fill in your chart by asking the appropriate questions.
- One student begins the conversation by making the statement on his or her card.

- The other student responds with questions until all three spaces on the chart have been filled in.

- Remember to use the language presented below and to take notes only. Do not write word-for-word what the other person says.

Sample Dialogue

A: Excuse me, what's your topic?

B: Universities

A: (Finds the topic on the chart.) Okay, go ahead.

B: As far as I'm concerned, it's best to choose a university based on the amenities it offers.

A: **You mentioned amenities. I was wondering if you could explain what that means.**

B: Yes, it's the pleasant or beneficial features of a place.

A: **Could you spell it, please?**

B: Yes. A-M-E-N-I-T-I-E-S

A: **And could you give me an example?**

B: Yes. A swimming pool is an amenity.

A: Thank you.

Key Language

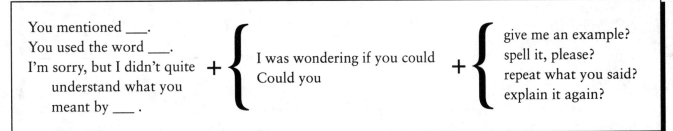

You mentioned ___.
You used the word ___.
I'm sorry, but I didn't quite understand what you meant by ___ .

+ { I was wondering if you could
Could you

+ { give me an example?
spell it, please?
repeat what you said?
explain it again?

TOPIC	NEW WORD	DEFINITION	EXAMPLE
Example: Universities	amenities	a place's fun or useful features	a swimming pool
1. Australia			
2. Biology			
3. Food			
4. Trees			
5. Jewelry			
6. Plants			
7. Survival			
8. Languages			
9. Animals			
10. Vegetables			
11. The Weather			
12. Buildings			

Before you actually give your presentation you should first practice it. Practicing your presentation in advance will make you more confident when it comes time to do "the real thing." It will also give you an opportunity to make any changes to your presentation or to your note cards before you begin. You can also check the length of your presentation to make sure that it is appropriate for the amount of time you have been given.

If you have time, practice your final presentation at home before giving it in class. To do this, you can use either a mirror or a tape recorder, or ask one of your friends or family members to listen and give you some feedback. Whichever method you choose, make sure that you time yourself to ensure that your presentation is within the five- to ten-minute range.

When giving your presentation, it is very important that you look up at your audience as much as possible. The first essential step in achieving this is to write effective note cards and to make sure that you can use them without looking at them constantly. Once you are in the classroom, make sure that you look at all parts of the audience. Do not look at the floor, and do not look at the wall above your audience.

When you are giving your presentation, make sure that you speak loudly enough so that everyone can hear what you are saying and slowly enough so that everyone can understand. Grammatical accuracy and clear pronunciation will also make it easier for the audience to understand your presentation. Finally, remember to explain any vocabulary that your audience may not understand.

> **PRACTICE 7: PRACTICING YOUR PRESENTATION**
>
> The purpose of Activity 11 is to give you the chance to practice your presentation in order to improve your organization and delivery.

Activity 11: Small Group Practice

- In this activity you will work in a group of four, made up of two pairs. When practicing, you will give your presentation to the whole group, but when giving and getting feedback you will work only with your partner.
- When giving your presentation, keep in mind the points mentioned above.
- Give feedback to one another by filling out the following checklist and adding any comments that you may have. If you would like a written copy of the feedback, then it might be a good idea to exchange books with your partner before you begin.
- After you have given your presentations and filled out the checklists, divide into your assigned pairs for the peer tutorial, which is the Unit Assignment from Unit Five.
- Remember to use the language for asking for and giving advice that we studied in Unit Five.

INFORMATION PRESENTATION CHECKLIST

Name of Speaker: _____

Name of Evaluator: _____

Presentation Topic: _____

Start Time: _____

After reading this checklist carefully, listen to the presentation and evaluate the speaker on each criterion. Put a ✓+ (excellent), ✓ (okay), or ✓− (needs improvement) in the space provided.

Content and Organization

Introduction

_____ Attracted the attention of the audience

_____ Stated the topic clearly

Body

_____ Organized ideas well

_____ Used appropriate expressions to "mark" the organization

_____ Provided adequate detail and examples

Conclusion

_____ Offered a final thought on the topic

_____ Used appropriate expressions for concluding a presentation

Delivery

_____ Used note cards effectively

_____ Made eye contact with the audience

_____ Spoke loudly

_____ Spoke fluently

_____ Spoke with grammatical accuracy

_____ Spoke with clear pronunciation

_____ Spoke at an appropriate speed

_____ Explained unfamiliar vocabulary

End Time: _____   *Length of Presentation:* _____

CHAPTER ASSIGNMENT: PRESENTING INFORMATION TO A SMALL GROUP

 Activity 12: Group Presentations

Presenter

As the final activity in this unit, you will be asked to give your information presentation to a group of two or three other students in the class. By now you should be well prepared, so relax and enjoy the experience.

Remember that your presentation should be five to ten minutes long, and that you should leave five minutes at the end of your presentation for questions. You may want to end your presentation with the words "Thank you. Do you have any questions?"

Listener

Your teacher may ask you to take notes on the presentations, using the note-taking sheets provided on the next page. This activity will help you to follow the main points of the presentation and to practice your note-taking skills. Good notes will enable you to remember the content of each presentation, to remember new vocabulary, and to participate in a discussion later on. Use your note-taking sheet as a source for questions; for example, if one section of your note-taking sheet is blank, ask a question about that section.

**Information Presentation:
Note-taking Sheet**

Name of Speaker: _____

Topic: _____

Introduction:

Body: (Main Points and Examples)

Conclusion:

Other:

**Information Presentation:
Note-taking Sheet**

Name of Speaker: _____

Topic: _____

Introduction:

Body: (Main Points and Examples)

Conclusion:

Other:

CHAPTER ELEVEN: *Summary of Key Language*

INTRODUCING A TOPIC

Today I'd like to talk about . . .

First I'd like to talk about . . .

The next . . . I'll talk about . . .

GIVING EXAMPLES

For example . . .

For instance . . .

To illustrate . . .

ORDERING INFORMATION

The first/second/third . . .

The next . . .

The last/final . . .

CONCLUDING A TOPIC

In conclusion . . .

In summary . . .

To conclude . . .

To sum up . . .

As I mentioned before . . .

QUESTIONING A SPEAKER

In your presentation you mentioned _____ .

I was wondering if you could give me an example.

I'm sorry, but I didn't quite understand what you meant by _____ .

Could you explain it again, please?

Could you please repeat what you said about _____ ?

In your presentation you used the word _____ . Could you spell that, please?

OTHER

Chapter Twelve

Demonstrating a Process to a Group

IN ORDER TO SUCCESSFULLY ATTACK A POSTMAN, YOU NEED THREE THINGS: A PLAN OF ATTACK, AN ESCAPE ROUTE, AND OF COURSE, A VICTIM! LET US BEGIN WITH THE CLASSIC VICTIM.

FIRSTLY, THE CLASSIC VICTIM WILL BE WEARING SHORTS, THUS ALLOWING FOR A BETTER GRIP ON THE LEG. FOR THIS REASON, ATTACKS IN SUMMER ARE PREFERABLE.

SECONDLY, THE CLASSIC VICTIM WILL BE CARRYING A HEAVY BAG AND HAVE BOTH HANDS FULL OF LETTERS OR PARCELS. THUS THE VICTIM WILL FIND IT DIFFICULT TO RUN AWAY AND WILL HAVE PROBLEMS DEFENDING HIMSELF OR HERSELF.

FINALLY, THE CLASSIC VICTIM WILL BE LISTENING TO A WALKMAN AND WILL THUS BE TOTALLY UNAWARE OF WHAT IS HAPPENING UNTIL THE MOMENT YOU ACTUALLY BITE THE LEG.

INTRODUCTION

In Chapter Eleven you learned how to present information to a small audience. In this chapter you will learn how to give a demonstration presentation to a larger group of people. In an information presentation, the speaker presents information on a specific topic. In a demonstration presentation, the speaker shows the audience how to do something. In other words, the focus of the demonstration presentation should be on *showing*, rather than *telling*.

 Activity 1: Brainstorming

1. What do you feel are the differences between giving a presentation to a small group and presenting in front of a large group?
2. When showing someone how to do something, what expressions might you use to help organize your ideas for the audience?

DIALOGUE ANALYSIS

 Activity 2: Gap-Filling

Listen to the student presentation and fill in the missing words in the tape-script below.

How to Put on Scuba Equipment

As you all know from last week's presentation, scuba diving has become an extremely popular sport in recent years. With increased advertising and flight availability to the more remote places on Earth, people are opting to take scuba diving vacations during both the summer and winter seasons. Some divers complete a scuba course prior to going on vacation, 5 while others choose to take a "resort course" after they arrive at their vacation destination. Whichever method of training you choose, one of the most basic skills you will learn is how to put on scuba equipment. **So, today I'm going to show you how to** put on scuba equipment correctly and efficiently. 10

To (1) _____ _____, make sure that you have all of your equipment in one area. The basic equipment that you will need is: a tank, a buoyancy compensator vest (BCV), a regulator, a weight belt, booties, gloves, a mask, snorkel, fins, and a wet suit.

The (2) _____ **step** is to put on your booties and wet suit. It is a good 15 idea to wet them first so that they will slide on more easily. **The (3)** _____ _____ is to attach the BCV to the tank. To do this, stand your tank up and fasten the BCV strap tightly around the belly of the tank. (4) _____ to lift the tank by the BCV handle to make sure that the tank does not slip. The third step is to attach the regulator to the tank. **It is** 20 (5) _____ _____ **that** this is done correctly since the regulator is the piece of equipment that will provide you with air. After it is attached, turn on the air and take a few breaths to make sure that the air flows at a comfortable rate and that it tastes clean. (6) _____ _____, lean forward and ask your buddy, the person you are diving with, to help you put 25 on your tank. (7) _____ _____ that he or she helps support you until you have fastened the buckles and have regained your balance. Press the automatic inflator so that some air goes into the BCV. This is important in case you are accidentally tossed into the water. With air in the BCV, you won't sink to the bottom, but will float on top. (8) _____, put on your 30 weight belt. (9) _____ put on your weight belt unless you have air in your BCV. Otherwise, you may sink to the bottom in an accident. (10) _____, put your mask and snorkel over your head with the snorkel on the left side. Walk over to your exact point of entry, put on your fins,

put your regulator in your mouth, put your mask on your face, steady the 35
regulator and your mask on your face with one hand and take the plunge!

Although putting on scuba equipment may look difficult if you have
never done it before, once you get used to it, it becomes a natural part of
the scuba diving experience. The most important thing is to have equipment that works reliably and fits properly. That is what makes scuba div- 40
ing so safe and pleasurable. **Thank you very much. Do you have (11)**
_____ _____?

At the end of Chapter Twelve, you will be asked to do a ten-minute demonstration presentation in front of the class. As mentioned before, the purpose
of a demonstration presentation is to *show* your classmates how to do
something.

The first step in giving a presentation is to choose a topic as you did for your
information presentation. Remember to consider the following criteria when
choosing a topic:

- It should be interesting to both you and your classmates.
- It should be specific enough to demonstrate in ten minutes.
- You must be able to actually demonstrate each step for your audience.
- You should not choose a topic that will make the members of your
  audience feel uncomfortable.
- You should not choose a topic that is too simple, for example, tying
  a shoe.
- You should not choose a topic that is too complicated, for example, how
  to build a computer.

When choosing your topic, try to think of ways that your audience can
participate and remember that you will need to bring in any necessary
supplies.

 **Activity 3: Small Group Discussion**

The following is a list of possible presentation topics. With the
above criteria in mind, discuss each topic with the other students in your group. Put an **X** next to the topics that would
not be appropriate and a ✓ next to the topics that would
be appropriate. In each case, justify your opinion and
explain how the topic might be improved.

Examples:

X **How to use a computer**
too complicated, too long, difficult to see, difficult to demonstrate: could be improved by limiting the topic to one specific area of computer use, such as demonstrating how to use a mouse. (e.g. scrolling, dragging, clicking, etc.) if an overhead computer monitor were available

X **How to tie your shoes**
too simple, too short, not interesting: difficult to improve

✓ **How to do a particular flower arrangement**
easy to see, interesting to many people, can be done in ten minutes, audience could participate

1. _____ How to play the guitar

_____

_____

_____

2. _____ How to do a particular dance step

_____

_____

_____

3. _____ How to read a book

_____

_____

_____

4. _____ How to make a greeting card

_____

_____

_____

5. _____ How to play soccer

_____

_____

6. ____ How to wash a car

_____

_____

_____

7. ____ How to clean a desk

_____

_____

_____

8. ____ How to make a simple toy

_____

_____

_____

9. ____ How to fly a kite

_____

_____

_____

10. ____ How to make toast

_____

_____

_____

Activity 4: Small Group Discussion

Now think of three possible topics for your demonstration presentation. List
them below, and then discuss each one with your partners.

1) _____

2) _____

3) _____

PRACTICE 2: USING VISUAL AIDS

The purpose of Activity 5 is to understand the advantages and disadvantages of various types of visual aids. This information will help you decide what visual aids to use in your presentation.

When choosing a topic, you should also consider what type of visual aids you will use. For a demonstration presentation in particular the visual aids you choose will, to a large extent, determine the success of your presentation.

 Activity 5: Brainstorming

In pairs or small groups, fill in the advantages and disadvantages of each of the following types of visual aids. The first one has been done for you.

	Advantages	Disadvantages
Blackboard/Whiteboard	big, visible, available	handwriting may be difficult to read, writing takes time during the presentation
Overhead Projector		
Video		
Flip-chart		
Handout		
Objects		
Your Body		
Pictures (posters/photographs)		
Diagrams/Graphs/Charts		

As we discussed earlier, doing a demonstration presentation involves describing how to do something. Thus, you will need to use the following expressions for *sequencing events and instructions.*

Key Language

First of all,
First, second, third, etc.
Next,
After that,
Then,
The first step, the second step, the final step
After you have (verb + ed), you should . . .
After (verb + ing), you should . . .

PRACTICE 3: DESCRIBING A PROCESS

The purpose of Activity 6 is to provide an opportunity for you to practice using the appropriate language for sequencing events and instructions.

Activity 6: Class Mingle

- Your teacher will give you a piece of paper with a square on it.
- The square represents six steps in a process.
- When completed, it will contain all the necessary instructions for making an object.
- Your task is to complete the square by collecting information from other students in the class.
- You may only collect information which follows the information you already have. For example, if you already have number 5, then you must find a student who has number 6. Once you have number 6, you must then find a student who has number 1, and so on until you have filled in all six steps.
- Each time you meet a new student you should read out the information you already have.
- If that person has the information that follows yours, he or she will tell you and you can write it down.
- If that person doesn't, then you should use a thanking expression and move on to a new student.
- When you have filled in all six steps, try to guess what object the instructions are for.

Activity 7: Class Mingle

For this activity, you will use the chart on the next page and a strip of paper that your teacher will give you. When you receive the paper, write the *plan* at the top of the page above the chart.

You have two tasks:
1. Complete the chart on the next page by asking other students to remind you of things you need to do.
2. Help other students to complete their charts by reminding them of things to do using the language in the box on the next page.

- Mingle with other students and find a partner.
- Read your plan and write down the reminder that your partner gives you.
- If another student has already given you that reminder, ask your partner for another one.

- Listen to your partner's plan.
- Think of an appropriate reminder that will help him or her accomplish that plan.
- Remind your partner, using one of the expressions given in the box at the bottom of the page.
- If your partner already has that information, suggest another reminder, using a different expression.
- When you have finished, mingle again and find another partner.

Activity 7: Chart

Plan: _____

Reminders:

1.

2.

3.

4.

5.

6.

Key Language

Reminding Someone to Do Something

It's important that you . . .	It's best to . . .
It's a good idea to . . .	Remember to . . .
It will be necessary to . . .	Don't forget to . . .
You will need/want to . . .	Never . . .
You should . . .	Make sure not to . . .

CHAPTER ASSIGNMENT: DEMONSTRATING A PROCESS TO A GROUP

Activity 8: Group Presentations

As the final activity in this unit, you will be asked to give a demonstration presentation to the class. Your teacher may ask the other students to take notes on the presentations, using the note taking sheets provided on the following pages. Use this opportunity to practice your note taking skills and to record the information from the presentations for future reference.

Remember to plan a fifteen-minute presentation (ten minutes to present and five minutes to answer questions). You may want to end your presentation with the words "Thank you. Do you have any questions?"

You should use visual aids during your presentation and speak from note cards. Aim for effective eye contact and posture. If possible, try to practice your presentation prior to actually doing it in front of the class. The Information Presentation checklist from Chapter Eleven (page 168) might prove useful again, as would a peer tutorial.

Activity 8: Note-taking Sheet

Demonstration Presentation: Note-taking Sheet

Name of Speaker: _____

Topic: _____

Introduction

Body (Main Steps of the Process)

Conclusion

Other:

Activity 8: Note-taking Sheet

Demonstration Presentation: Note-taking Sheet

Name of Speaker: _____

Topic: _____

Introduction

Body (Main Steps of the Process)

Conclusion

Other:

CHAPTER TWELVE: *Summary of Key Language*

SEQUENCING EVENTS OR INSTRUCTIONS

First of all,

First, second, third, etc.

Next,

After that,

Then,

The first step, the second step, the final step

After you have (verb + ed), you should . . .

After (verb + ing), you should . . .

REMINDING SOMEONE TO DO SOMETHING

It's important that you . . .

It's a good idea to . . .

It will be necessary to . . .

You will need/want to . . .

You should . . .

It's best to . . .

Remember to . . .

Don't forget to . . .

Never . . .

Make sure not to . . .

OTHER

Chapter Thirteen

Planning a Group Project

INTRODUCTION

At some time during your studies, you may be required to do a group project. A group project is any project that requires students to work together to complete a group assignment. A group project may be a written assignment, an oral presentation, or some other type of assignment, such as an art project or drama performance. One measure of a successful group project is whether all group members work together cooperatively and effectively. This chapter focuses on how to plan a group project. It will cover strategies for making suggestions, volunteering to help, and asking for volunteers.

 **Activity 1: Small Group Discussion**

1. Have you ever been required to do a group project in your own language or in English? If so, what difficulties, if any, did you encounter?

2. What suggestions for success, if any, do you have for students working on a group project in English?

DIALOGUE ANALYSIS

 Activity 2: Gap-Filling

Look at the expressions for *asking for volunteers, making suggestions,* and *volunteering to help* at the end of the dialogue. Next, listen to the dialogue once for a general understanding. Then, listen to the dialogue again and, in the spaces provided, fill in the letters that correspond to the expressions you hear for *making suggestions, volunteering to help,* and *asking for volunteers.*

Father: . . . so, that's the situation. Bill and Vera want to get married next week, but her parents don't even like our Billy, never mind letting their precious daughter get married to him with only one week's notice!

Mother: So, what are we going to do?   5

Father: _____ arrange the wedding ourselves?

Brother: But there are only five of us!

Sister: Well, we'll have to work as a team then, won't we?

Mother: All right, _____?

Sister: _____ do the catering.   10

Mother: That's very kind of you, but _____ more than one person doing all the cooking.

Brother: _____ helping. I enjoy cooking.

Sister: Well, _____ make the wedding cake.

Mother: Okay, that sounds great. Now, where are we going 15 to have the reception?

Father: _____ have it here. It would save money!

Mother: Don't be stupid. There isn't enough room.

(The telephone rings.)

Uncle: Well, _____ having it at the church 20 hall? It's convenient and cheap.

Mother: And it's probably all we can get on such short notice.

Uncle: Well, _____ phone the priest and see if it's available?   25

Mother: Yes, and _____ providing our own drinks.

Uncle: Well, _____ deal with the church hall and the drinks, then.

Mother: Okay. So, _____ getting Billy to the church on ₃₀ time?

Brother: _____ doing that.

Mother: Now, _____ hiring a mini-bus.

Father: Don't bother. That was Billy on the phone. They've eloped. They got married two hours ago! ₃₅

Asking for Volunteers
A. How should we divide the work?
B. Who wants/would like to . . . ?
C. Who wants/would like to be responsible for . . . ?

Making Suggestions
D. Why don't we . . . ?
E. How about . . . ?
F. We could . . .
G. We might want to . . .
H. Perhaps we should consider/think about . . .
I. We may want to consider/think about . . .
J. I'd like to suggest/propose that we . . .

Volunteering to Help
K. I wouldn't mind . . .
L. I'd be happy to . . .
M. I could . . .
N. Why don't I . . . ?
O. I don't mind . . .

PRACTICE 1: MAKING SUGGESTIONS

The purpose of Activity 3 is to practice making suggestions.

 ## Activity 3: Fluency Circles

- Your teacher will give you a strip of paper with a statement on it.
- First, learn the statement.
- Then, your teacher will ask you and your classmates to form two circles, one inside the other, with each student facing a partner.

- To begin, the student on the outside circle states the idea on the strip of paper.
- The partner on the inside circle responds with a suggestion, using one of the expressions listed below.
- Next, the partner on the inside circle states the idea on his or her paper.
- The partner on the outside circle responds with a suggestion, using one of the expressions below.
- After you and your partner have each made a suggestion, your teacher will ask you to move on to a new partner.

REMEMBER
- Try not to look at your statement while you are talking.
- Try to use the expressions that you are least familiar with.

Sample Dialogue

> A: **The weather is terrible today, isn't it?**
> B: Yes it is. **Perhaps we should consider** staying inside.
> A: Yes, that's a good idea.

Key Language

> *Making Suggestions*
> Why don't we . . . ?
> How about + (verb) + ing?
> We could . . .
> We might want to . . .
> Perhaps we should consider/think about + (verb) + ing.
> We may want to consider/think about + (verb) + ing.
> I'd like to suggest/propose that we . . .

Activity 4: Groupwork

STUDENT A

- For this activity you will work in groups of three.
- Your task is to listen to the other students' problems and to volunteer to help them.
- To begin, Student A reads the first problem and the other two students volunteer to help.
- Try to volunteer to help as many times and in as many ways as you can.
- When Students B and C can't think of any more ways to volunteer, Student B reads out a statement and the other two volunteer to help, and so on.
- The student who volunteers the most wins the game.
- To keep count, each time you volunteer, put a check mark next to the problem listed at the bottom of this page.

Sample Dialogue

Student A:	I have so much housework to do tonight, I don't know how I'll ever get to sleep!
Student B:	**I'd be happy to** help you do the dishes.
Student C:	**I wouldn't mind** sweeping the floor.
Student B:	**I could** wash the windows.
Student C:	**Why don't I** cook dinner?

- Remember to use the expressions for volunteering to help!!!

PROBLEMS:
1. I'm moving in three weeks, and I have so much to do!
2. I'm in charge of the school picnic, and I don't know how I'm going to get everything done!

NUMBER OF TIMES I VOLUNTEERED:

STUDENT B	STUDENT C
1. Getting Married:	1. Going on Vacation:
2. Brother's Coming to Visit:	2. Having a Big Party:

PRACTICE 2: VOLUNTEERING TO HELP

The purpose of Activity 4 is to practice volunteering to help.

 Activity 4: Groupwork

STUDENT B

- For this activity you will work in groups of three.
- Your task is to listen to the other students' problems and to volunteer to help them.
- To begin, Student A reads the first problem and the other two students volunteer to help.
- Try to volunteer to help as many times and in as many ways as you can.
- When Students B and C can't think of any more ways to volunteer, Student B reads out a statement and the other two volunteer to help, and so on.
- The student who volunteers the most wins the game.
- To keep count, each time you volunteer, put a check mark next to the problem listed at the bottom of this page.

Sample Dialogue

Student A:	I have so much housework to do tonight, I don't know how I'll ever get to sleep!
Student B:	**I'd be happy to** help you do the dishes.
Student C:	**I wouldn't mind** sweeping the floor.
Student B:	**I could** wash the windows.
Student C:	**Why don't I** cook dinner?

- Remember to use the expressions for volunteering to help!!!

PROBLEMS:

1. I'm getting married in two months, and I have so much to do!
2. My brother is coming to visit next week, and I don't know how I'm going to get everything ready in time!

NUMBER OF TIMES I VOLUNTEERED:

STUDENT A	STUDENT C
1. Moving Soon:	1. Going on Vacation:
2. In Charge of the School Picnic:	2. Having a Big Party:

Activity 4: Groupwork

STUDENT C

- For this activity you will work in groups of three.
- Your task is to listen to the other students' problems and to volunteer to help them.
- To begin, Student A reads the first problem and the other two students volunteer to help.
- Try to volunteer to help as many times and in as many ways as you can.
- When Students B and C can't think of any more ways to volunteer, Student B reads out a statement and the other two volunteer to help, and so on.
- The student who volunteers the most wins the game.
- To keep count, each time you volunteer, put a check mark next to the problem listed at the bottom of this page.

> **PRACTICE 2: VOLUNTEERING TO HELP**
>
> The purpose of Activity 4 is to practice volunteering to help.

Sample Dialogue

Student A:	I have so much housework to do tonight, I don't know how I'll ever get to sleep!
Student B:	**I'd be happy to** help you do the dishes.
Student C:	**I wouldn't mind** sweeping the floor.
Student B:	**I could** wash the windows.
Student C:	**Why don't I** cook dinner?

- Remember to use the expressions for volunteering to help!!!

PROBLEMS:
1. Next week, I'm going on a two-week vacation, and I'm worried that I won't have enough time to get ready!
2. I'm having a big party this week, and I have so much to do!

NUMBER OF TIMES I VOLUNTEERED:

STUDENT A	STUDENT B
1. Moving Soon:	1. Getting Married
2. In Charge of the School Picnic:	2. Brother's Coming to Visit:

PRACTICE 3: ASKING FOR VOLUNTEERS

The purpose of Activity 5 is to practice asking other people in your group to volunteer help.

 Activity 5: Group Bingo

For this activity you will work in groups of four. The activity is a form of bingo, with the winner being the person who completes his or her Volunteer Bingo Card first. During the activity you will take turns at being the "bingo caller." When you are not the caller you are a player.

- Student A begins as the caller and asks for volunteers by choosing one of the tasks from the Work to Be Done list.
- The person who has that particular task on his or her Volunteer Bingo Card must volunteer to do the task and then cross the task off the card.
- The caller and the other two students should also cross the task off their Work to Be Done lists, so that it is not called out again.
- The person who had the task on the bingo card then becomes the caller and asks for volunteers by choosing a task from the Work to Be Done list.
- The activity continues until somebody crosses all the tasks off the bingo card, at which point they shout BINGO!
- Read the Sample Dialogue below. Then practice it with another member of your group before you begin the game.

Sample Dialogue

Student A:	Now, **how should we divide up the work?** Er, let's see . . . (Chooses one task from the Work to Be Done list) **Who wants to be responsible for** looking after the money?
Student D:	**I wouldn't mind** doing that.
Student D:	**Who would like to** cut the grass?
Student C:	**I'd be happy to** do it.

Activity 5: STUDENT A

Group Bingo Card

clean the kitchen	wash the dishes	taking notes	be the group leader
making a dessert	bring a computer	calling a taxi	carry the suitcase

Work to Be Done

- . . . go to the flower shop
- . . . buying a book
- . . . fix the copy machine
- . . . sending the fax
- . . . repair the bicycle
- . . . go to the bank
- . . . send a letter
- . . . sharpening the pencils

- . . . empty the trash can
- . . . wash the car
- . . . buying the stamps
- . . . getting the drinks
- . . . go to the library
- . . . answering the phone
- . . . fetch the tape recorder
- . . . buying the newspaper

- . . . watering the plants
- . . . writing the postcards
- . . . walk the dog
- . . . bring a camera
- . . . clean the room
- . . . feeding the cat
- . . . buying the present
- . . . make the coffee

When you are the caller, remember to use the language for *Asking for Volunteers,* and when volunteering use the language for *Volunteering to Help.* Make sure that you use an expression that agrees with the verb form given on the bingo card.

Key Language

Asking for Volunteers	*Volunteering to Help*
How should we divide the work?	I wouldn't mind . . . ing . . .
Who wants to . . . ?	I'd be happy to . . .
Who would like to . . . ?	I could . . .
Who wants to be responsible for . . . ing . . . ?	Why don't I . . . ?
Who would like to be responsible for . . . ing . . . ?	I don't mind . . . ing . . .

Activity 5: STUDENT B

Group Bingo Card

send a letter	sending the fax	go to the bank	sharpening the pencils
buying a book	fix the copy machine	repair the bicycle	go to the flower shop

Work to Be Done

- . . . wash the car
- . . . buying the stamps
- . . . getting the drinks
- . . . go to the library
- . . . answering the phone
- . . . fetch the tape recorder
- . . . buying the newspaper
- . . . watering the plants

- . . . writing the postcards
- . . . walk the dog
- . . . bring a camera
- . . . clean the room
- . . . feeding the cat
- . . . buying the present
- . . . make the coffee
- . . . bring a computer

- . . . calling a taxi
- . . . be the group leader
- . . . making a dessert
- . . . taking notes
- . . . carry the suitcase
- . . . clean the kitchen
- . . . wash the dishes
- . . . empty the trash can

When you are the caller, remember to use the language for *Asking for Volunteers,* and when volunteering use the language for *Volunteering to Help.* Make sure that you use an expression that agrees with the verb form given on the bingo card.

Key Language

Asking for Volunteers	*Volunteering to Help*
How should we divide the work?	I wouldn't mind . . . ing . . .
Who wants to . . . ?	I'd be happy to . . .
Who would like to . . . ?	I could . . .
Who wants to be responsible for . . . ing . . . ?	Why don't I . . . ?
Who would like to be responsible for . . . ing . . . ?	I don't mind . . . ing . . .

Activity 5: STUDENT C

Group Bingo Card

watering the plants	writing the postcards	bring a camera	feeding the cat
walk the dog	buying the present	clean the room	make the coffee

Work to Be Done

- . . . go to the flower shop
- . . . buying a book
- . . . fix the copy machine
- . . . sending the fax
- . . . repair the bicycle
- . . . go to the bank
- . . . send a letter
- . . . sharpening the pencils

- . . . empty the trash can
- . . . wash the car
- . . . buying the stamps
- . . . getting the drinks
- . . . go to the library
- . . . answering the phone
- . . . fetch the tape recorder
- . . . buying the newspaper

- . . . calling a taxi
- . . . be the group leader
- . . . making a dessert
- . . . taking notes
- . . . carry the suitcase
- . . . clean the kitchen
- . . . wash the dishes
- . . . bring a computer

When you are the caller, remember to use the language for *Asking for Volunteers,* and when volunteering use the language for *Volunteering to Help.* Make sure that you use an expression that agrees with the verb form given on the bingo card.

Key Language

Asking for Volunteers	*Volunteering to Help*
How should we divide the work?	I wouldn't mind . . . ing . . .
Who wants to . . . ?	I'd be happy to . . .
Who would like to . . . ?	I could . . .
Who wants to be responsible for . . . ing . . . ?	Why don't I . . . ?
Who would like to be responsible for . . . ing . . . ?	I don't mind . . . ing . . .

Activity 5: STUDENT D

Group Bingo Card

go to the library	getting the drinks	answering the phone	fetch the tape recorder
wash the car	buying the stamps	buying the newspaper	empty the trash can

Work to Be Done

- . . . go to the flower shop
- . . . buying a book
- . . . fix the copy machine
- . . . sending the fax
- . . . repair the bicycle
- . . . go to the bank
- . . . send a letter
- . . . sharpening the pencils

- . . . carry the suitcase
- . . . making a dessert
- . . . calling a taxi
- . . . taking notes
- . . . clean the kitchen
- . . . wash the dishes
- . . . be the group leader
- . . . bring a computer

- . . . watering the plants
- . . . writing the postcards
- . . . walk the dog
- . . . bring a camera
- . . . clean the room
- . . . feeding the cat
- . . . buying the present
- . . . make the coffee

When you are the caller, remember to use the language for *Asking for Volunteers*, and when volunteering use the language for *Volunteering to Help*. Make sure that you use an expression that agrees with the verb form given on the bingo card.

Key Language

Asking for Volunteers	*Volunteering to Help*
How should we divide the work?	I wouldn't mind . . . ing . . .
Who wants to . . . ?	I'd be happy to . . .
Who would like to . . . ?	I could . . .
Who wants to be responsible for . . . ing . . . ?	Why don't I . . . ?
Who would like to be responsible for . . . ing . . . ?	I don't mind . . . ing . . .

CHAPTER ASSIGNMENT: PLANNING A GROUP PROJECT

Activity 6: Role Play   STUDENT A

Activity 6 consists of three role plays. In the first role play you will play the project leader, and in the second and third you will be a participant. Try to do the role plays without looking at the key language on the right side of the page. If you finish before the other groups, change role sheets and begin again.

ROLE ONE: THE PROJECT LEADER

Your teacher has asked your group to act out a story to the class. To do this, you must:

- write the story
- choose the role that each student will play
- schedule your practice sessions
- choose costumes
- arrange your "stage"
- other?

Decide how you will do it, and divide the work equally among all group members.

- Remember to use the appropriate expressions for making suggestions, volunteering to help, and asking for volunteers.

KEY LANGUAGE:

Asking for Volunteers
How should we divide the work?
Who wants/would like to . . . ?
Who wants/would like to be responsible for . . . ?

ROLE TWO: A PARTICIPANT

Listen to the task presented by the project leader. Discuss the project, making suggestions and volunteering to help whenever you can.

KEY LANGUAGE:

Making Suggestions
Why don't we . . . ?
How about . . . ?
We could . . .
We might want to . . .
Perhaps we should consider/think about . . .
We may want to consider/think about . . .
I'd like to suggest/propose that we . . .

Volunteering to Help
I wouldn't mind . . .
I'd be happy to . . .
I could . . .
Why don't I . . . ?
I don't mind . . .

ROLE THREE: A PARTICIPANT

Listen to the task presented by the project leader. Discuss the project, making suggestions and volunteering to help whenever you can.

KEY LANGUAGE:

(See Role Two above.)

CHAPTER ASSIGNMENT: PLANNING A GROUP PROJECT

Activity 6: Role Play   STUDENT B

Activity 6 consists of three role plays. In the first and third you will be a participant, and in the second you will play the project leader. Try to do the role plays without looking at the key language on the right side of the page. If you finish before the other groups, change role sheets and begin again.

ROLE ONE: A PARTICIPANT	
Listen to the task presented by the project leader. Discuss the project, making suggestions and volunteering to help whenever you can.	**KEY LANGUAGE:** **Making Suggestions** Why don't we . . . ? How about . . . ? We could . . . We might want to . . . Perhaps we should consider/think about . . . We may want to consider/think about . . . I'd like to suggest/propose that we . . . **Volunteering to Help** I wouldn't mind . . . I'd be happy to . . . I could . . . Why don't I . . . ? I don't mind . . .
ROLE TWO: THE PROJECT LEADER	
Your teacher has asked your group to hand in a written report on a country of your choice. To do this, you must: • choose which country you will report on • decide which aspect of the country you will report on • schedule your work sessions • decide who will write each part • decide how you will put it all together • other? Decide how you will do it, and divide the work equally among all group members.	• Remember to use the appropriate expressions for making suggestions, volunteering to help, and asking for volunteers. **KEY LANGUAGE:** **Asking for Volunteers** How should we divide the work? Who wants/would like to . . . ? Who wants/would like to be responsible for . . . ?
ROLE THREE: A PARTICIPANT	
Listen to the task presented by the project leader. Discuss the project, making suggestions and volunteering to help whenever you can.	**KEY LANGUAGE:** (See Role One above.)

CHAPTER ASSIGNMENT: PLANNING A GROUP PROJECT

 Activity 6: Role Play   **STUDENT C**

Activity 6 consists of three role plays. In the first and second you will be a participant, and in the third you will play the project leader. Try to do the role plays without looking at the key language on the right side of the page. If you finish before the other groups, change role sheets and begin again.

ROLE ONE: A PARTICIPANT	
Listen to the task presented by the project leader. Discuss the project, making suggestions and volunteering to help whenever you can.	KEY LANGUAGE: **Making Suggestions** Why don't we . . .? How about . . .? We could . . . We might want to . . . Perhaps we should consider/think about . . . We may want to consider/think about . . . I'd like to suggest/propose that we . . . **Volunteering to Help** I wouldn't mind . . . I'd be happy to . . . I could . . . Why don't I . . . ? I don't mind . . .

ROLE TWO: A PARTICIPANT	
Listen to the task presented by the project leader. Discuss the project, making suggestions and volunteering to help whenever you can.	KEY LANGUAGE: (See Role One above.)

ROLE THREE: THE PROJECT LEADER	
Your teacher has asked your group do a presentation in front of the class. To do this, you must: • choose a topic • choose the part that each student will present • schedule your work sessions • decide where you will get your information • decide what visual aids you will bring • other? Decide how you will do it, and divide the work equally among all group members.	• Remember to use the appropriate expressions for making suggestions, volunteering to help, and asking for volunteers. KEY LANGUAGE: **Asking for Volunteers** How should we divide the work? Who wants/would like to . . . ? Who wants/would like to be responsible for . . . ?

CHAPTER THIRTEEN: *Summary of Key Language*

MAKING SUGGESTIONS

Why don't we . . . ?

How about . . . ?

We could . . .

We might want to . . .

Perhaps we should consider/think about . . .

We may want to consider/think about . . .

I'd like to suggest/propose that we . . .

VOLUNTEERING TO HELP

I wouldn't mind . . .

I'd be happy to . . .

I could . . .

Why don't I . . . ?

I don't mind . . .

ASKING FOR VOLUNTEERS

How should we divide the work?

Who wants to . . . ?

Who would like to . . . ?

Who wants to be responsible for . . . ing?

Who would like to be responsible for . . . ing?

OTHER

UNIT ASSIGNMENT: THE GROUP PROJECT

As the final activity for this unit, you will do a group presentation in front of the class. When preparing the presentation you must:

- choose an appropriate topic
- get your teacher's permission to use the topic you have chosen
- write an introduction, body, and conclusion
- get information from outside sources, such as the library or a survey that you design
- decide who will present which parts of the presentation
- practice together

When giving the presentation, you must:

- each speak for an equal amount of time
- use note cards
- use visual aids

Suggested Procedure

1. Brainstorm topics and decide what visual aids you will use.
2. Choose what source(s) you will use, and write a survey if necessary.
3. Do your library research or conduct your survey.
4. Analyze your data.
5. Prepare your presentation.
6. Prepare your visual aids.
7. Decide who will speak on which part.
8. Make your note cards.
9. Practice.
10. Give your presentation.

Listening Task

While your classmates are giving their presentations, listen carefully and take notes on any interesting information that you would like to remember or discuss later. Your teacher may give you an opportunity to meet with the students from other groups to discuss each topic in more detail.

INDEX OF KEY LANGUAGE

Agreeing   *Chapter Seven*
    Yes, I see what you mean.
    That's true.
    I agree.
    Yes, maybe you're right.
    Yes, I think so too.
    I completely agree.
    Exactly!

Apologizing   *Chapter Six*
    I'm (very/really/awfully) sorry.

Asking for Advice   *Chapter Ten*
    What do you think I should do?
    What do you suggest I do?
    What do you recommend I do?
    What should I do?

Asking for a Definition   *Chapter Three*
    What does _____ mean?
    Excuse me, what is the meaning of _____ ?
    I'm not sure what you mean.
    I'm sorry, but I don't understand what you mean.
    Could you explain what you mean by _____ ?
    Could you give me an example?

Asking for an Opinion   *Chapter Eight*
    What about . . .?
    How about . . . ?
    What do you think, [name]?
    What do you think about that?
    Would anybody like to add to what [name] has just said?
    Would anybody like to comment on what [name] has just said?
    Does anybody have anything else to add?
    [Name], what's your opinion of . . . ?

Asking Permission　　　　　　　　　　　　　　　　　　　　　　*Chapter Six*
　Can I . . . ?
　Could I . . . ?
　Do you mind if I . . . ?
　Is it all right to . . . ?
　Would it be possible for me to . . . ?

Asking for Repetition　　　　　　　　　　　　　　　　　　　*Chapter Three*
　Could you repeat that, please?
　Excuse me, could you please repeat that from the beginning?
　Pardon me, could you please repeat the last sentence?
　Could you speak more slowly, please?

Asking for Volunteers　　　　　　　　　　　　　　　　　　*Chapter Thirteen*
　How should we divide the work?
　Who wants to . . . ?
　Who would like to . . . ?
　Who wants to be responsible for . . . ing?
　Who would like to be responsible for . . . ing?

Checking Spelling, Pronunciation, or Grammar　　　　　　　　*Chapter Three*
　Could you spell that, please?
　Could you pronounce this word, please?
　How do you spell that?
　How do you pronounce this word?
　What part of speech is that?

Closing a Conversation　(Making an appointment)　　　　　　　　*Chapter Five*
　Thank you very much. I'll see you then.

Closing a Conversation　(Visiting a teacher's office)　　　　　　　*Chapter Six*
　Well, thank you very much for your time.
　Well, I know you're busy. Thanks for your time.

Concluding a Report　　　　　　　　　　　　　　　　　　　*Chapter Nine*
　We came to the conclusion that . . .
　We decided that . . .
　Thank you.

Concluding a Topic

In conclusion . . .

In summary . . .

To conclude . . .

To sum up . . .

As I mentioned before . . .

Disagreeing

Yes, but . . .

I agree, but . . .

That may be, but . . .

You may be right, but . . .

I see your point, but . . .

Yes, but don't you think that . . . ?

Yes, but you have to remember that . . .

I don't quite agree. What about . . . ?

I'm not so sure I agree. I . . .

You (both) have a point, but . . .

Giving Advice

Chapter Ten

I always . . .

Sometimes I . . .

If I were you, I'd . . .

How about . . . ?

You might try . . .

You may want to . . .

Maybe you could . . .

It might be a good idea to . . .

Have you ever thought about . . .?

One thing I'd recommend is . . .

Another thing I'd recommend is . . .

Giving Examples

For example . . .

For instance . . .

To illustrate . . .

Giving an Opinion   *Chapter Seven*

    I think . . .

    I feel . . .

    It seems to me that . . .

    As far as I'm concerned . . .

    In my opinion . . .

Giving Reasons   *Chapter Six*

    . . . but . . . (I have/had to) . . .

    . . . because . . . (I have/had to) . . .

Interrupting   *Chapter One*

    Excuse me . . .

    Excuse me for interrupting, but . . .

    I'm sorry to interrupt, but . . .

    May I interrupt you for a moment?

    Excuse me. I hope you don't mind me interrupting, but . . .

Introducing Oneself   *Chapter One*

    Hi. My name's _____ .

    Hello. My name's _____.

    How do you do? My name's _____ .

    I'm _____ .

    Pleased to meet you.

    Nice to meet you (too).

Introducing a Topic   (Asking for information)   *Chapter Two*

    I'd like some information on/about . . .

    Do you have any information on/about . . .

    Could you tell me about . . .

    I'm interested in _____ . Do you have any information on that?

    I was wondering if you had any information on/about . . .

    I was wondering if you could tell me about . . .

Introducing a Topic   (Leading a group discussion)   *Chapter Eight*

    Today/First/Second we need to discuss/decide/prepare . . .

    Let's begin with . . .

Introducing a Topic (Presenting information to a small group)   *Chapter Eleven*
    Today I'd like to talk about . . .
    First I'd like to talk about . . .
    The next . . . I'll talk about . . .

Introducing a Topic (Reporting on a group discussion)   *Chapter Nine*
    On the topic of _____ we . . .
    On the subject of _____ we . . .
    In our discussion we talked about . . .
    We were trying to decide . . .
    We discussed . . .

Making an Appointment   *Chapter Five*
    I'd like to make an appointment to see you.
    I'd like to make an appointment to discuss . . .
    Could I make an appointment to talk about . . . ?
    Could I make an appointment to see you?

Making Suggestions   *Chapter Thirteen*
    Why don't we . . . ?
    How about . . . ?
    We could . . .
    We might want to . . .
    Perhaps we should consider/think about . . .
    We may want to consider/think about . . .
    I'd like to suggest/propose that we . . .

Moving on to a New Topic   *Chapter Eight*
    Okay, so we're all agreed that . . .
    Okay, so we all agree that . . .
    Okay, do we all agree that . . . ?
    Okay, let's move on to the next point.

Negotiating a Time   *Chapter Five*
    What time would be convenient for you?
    Are you free at . . . ?
    How about . . . ?
    What about . . . ?
    I'm sorry, but I'm busy at that time.
    Yes, that's fine.

Nonverbal Feedback   *Chapter Four*
    Nodding
    Smiling
    Eye contact
    Note-taking
    Body language

Opening a Conversation   *Chapters Five & Six*
    Excuse me, but do you have a minute?
    I'm sorry to bother you, but do you have a minute?
    Excuse me for interrupting, but could I talk to you for a minute?

Ordering Information   *Chapter Eleven*
    The first/second/third . . .
    The next . . .
    The last/final . . .

Paraphrasing to Confirm Meaning   *Chapter Three*
    Did you say . . . ?
    Do you mean . . . ?
    Are you saying that . . . ?

Questioning a Speaker   *Chapter Eleven*
    In your presentation you mentioned ____ . I was wondering if you could
        give me an example.
    I'm sorry, but I didn't quite understand what you meant by ____ .
        Could you explain it again, please?
    Could you please repeat what you said about ____ ?
    In your presentation you used the word ____ . Could you spell that, please?

Reminding Someone to Do Something   *Chapter Twelve*
    It's important that you . . .
    It's a good idea to . . .
    It will be necessary to . . .
    You will need/want to . . .
    You should . . .
    It's best to . . .
    Remember to . . .
    Don't forget to . . .
    Never . . .
    Make sure not to . . .

Reporting Information Chapter One

Have you heard (that) . . . ?
Did you hear (that) . . . ?
Do you know (that) . . . ?
Did you know (that) . . . ?
I heard (that) . . . .

Reporting Opinions Chapter Nine

_____ thought that . . .
_____ argued that . . .
_____ added that . . .
_____ suggested that . . .
_____ put forward the idea that . . .
This was supported by _____

Responding Chapter Eight

That's an interesting point/idea/opinion.
Yes, that's a good point.
I never thought of that.

Sequencing Events or Instructions Chapter Twelve

First of all,
First, second, third, etc.
Next,
After that,
Then,
The first step, the second step, the final step
After you have (verb + ed), you should . . .
After (verb + ing), you should . . .

Starting a Conversation Chapter One

Talking about the weather
Giving a compliment
Referring to a common situation

Stating One's Business Chapter Six

I'd like to talk to you about . . .
I have a small problem I'd like to discuss with you.
I'd like to ask your advice on something.

Summarizing   *Chapter Eight*

    Okay, so far we've said . . .

    Okay, so far we have . . .

    To sum up, we've said . . .

    Well, there seems to be some disagreement there.

Tag Responses   *Chapter Four*

    Did she?

    Are you?

    Were they?

    Has she?

    Will he?

Taking One's Leave   *Chapter One*

    Look at your watch. Give a reason.

    Mention the time. Give a reason.

    Ask for the time. (Answer) Give a reason.

+ {
  It's been nice talking with you.
  It's been a pleasure talking with you.
  I've really enjoyed talking with you.
}

Thanking   *Chapter Two*

    Thanks.

    Thank you.

    Thank you very much.

    Thank you very much for your time.

    Thank you. You've been very helpful.

    Thank you for taking the time to talk with me. I really appreciate it.

    Thanks anyway.

    Thank you anyway.

Verbal Feedback   *Chapter Four*

    Oh, really?

    Really?

    I see.

    Mmm.

    Uh huh.

Volunteering to Help   *Chapter Thirteen*

    I wouldn't mind . . .

    I'd be happy to . . .

    I could . . .

    Why don't I . . .?

    I don't mind . . .

Wh- questions

Who . . .?

What . . . ?

Where . . . ?

When . . . ?

Why . . . ?

How . . . ?

Yes–no Questions

Chapter Two

Can I keep my pet cat in the dorm?

Is there a bank on campus?

Do you have any brochures on study abroad programs?